NEIL YOUNG

The Reverb series looks at the connections between music, artists and performers, musical cultures and places. It explores how our cultural and historical understanding of times and places may help us to appreciate a wide variety of music, and vice versa.

reverb-series.co.uk
Series editor: John Scanlan

NEIL YOUNG

AMERICAN TRAVELLER

MARTIN HALLIWELL

REAKTION BOOKS

To Alex

Published by Reaktion Books Ltd
Unit 32, Waterside
44–48 Wharf Road
London N1 7UX, UK
www.reaktionbooks.co.uk

First published 2015

Printed and bound in Great Britain
by Bell & Bain, Glasgow

A catalogue record for this book is available from the British Library

ISBN 978 1 78023 531 8

CONTENTS

PREFACE

The three most listened-to albums of my undergraduate years spent in Devon in southwest England were *Freedom*, *Ragged Glory* and *Harvest Moon*. These were widely hailed as Neil Young's return to form after the uneven studio experiments of the 1980s when he was unhappily on the Geffen record label, and I felt lucky to be initiated into three dimensions of his music – the conceptual richness of *Freedom*, the heavy guitar grind of Crazy Horse on *Ragged Glory* and the lyrical nostalgia of *Harvest Moon* – but also saddened that this was not twenty years earlier, when the 'silver spaceships' of Young's countercultural song 'After the Gold Rush' might have transported me into a transcendent realm.

I often regretted that the year I was born, 1970, was not my coming-of-age year; that the increasingly corporate 1980s couldn't be traded in for the cultural vibrancy of the late 1960s; and that my student war (the Gulf War of 1990–91) did not harness the same energies of protest and creativity as the much longer war in Vietnam, even if it did spark Young's emotionally charged performances on his 1991 tour with Crazy Horse. Born a month after the Kent State University shootings by the National Guard of 4 May 1970 and the writing of Young's iconic protest song 'Ohio', I often felt like I was living at one remove from history, especially when the French theorist Jean Baudrillard was proclaiming that the Gulf War was only a virtual media spectacle for most people around the world. I even wondered how things might have been had I grown up in Seattle, where I lived as a small child in the early 1970s when my father was seconded there with Boeing. Too young to be aware of the gravity of the Watergate scandal or to know that Young's roadie Bruce Berry had been found dead from a heroin and cocaine overdose on my third birthday, I was more interested in hanging out with Disney characters in Anaheim or seeing totem poles in Vancouver.

A decade on, and back in the UK as a secondary-school kid in the East Midlands at a time when both progressive rock and punk had worn themselves out, I wanted to believe that being educated in the Pacific Northwest would have connected me to a more vibrant and politicized music scene than anything that was available in Britain. Of course, given my age and Seattle location, I would be much more likely to have been a Queensrÿche groupie or a Nirvana dropout than a devotee of Californian folk rock, even though Young performed live in Seattle four times between 1989 and 1992 (coinciding with my undergraduate years) and recorded his *Mirror Ball* album there with Pearl Jam in 1995.

For the most part, being British did not help my sense of connectedness, and perhaps led me to focus on American Studies as a graduate student in the mid-1990s, by which time I had filled in my missing years with most of Young's 1970s back catalogue. Two memorable moments from back then are waking up blearily at my parents' house halfway through the extended guitar solo of 'Cortez the Killer' to find that a cassette of Young and Crazy Horse's 1975 album *Zuma* had been playing on loop all night, and, a year later, going vinyl shopping with friends in Nottingham and triumphantly discovering a solitary German-import CD of Young's arguably most significant album, *On the Beach* (otherwise unavailable on CD at that time), in a now sadly closed record store, Selectadisc (1966–2009). There are many instances since when Young's music has been bound up with personal experiences in which place and time have been particularly resonant. My other major Canadian musical influence, Rush, rarely evoke geography in the same way, other than the occasional critique of suburban life (on their 1982 track 'Subdivisions') or reminiscing about growing up by the shore of Lake Ontario (on 'Lakeside Park' from 1975). Rush's lyricist Neil Peart is more often interested in metaphysical abstractions, scientific themes and alternative cosmologies than a rootedness in distinct North American locations. In contrast, on listening to Neil Young's music I discover moments and spaces that are both real and mythical.

I am very aware that my autobiographical 'sense of elsewhere' colours my response to songs such as 'Helpless' and 'Don't be Denied', through which Young reflects on his childhood and school years in Ontario and Manitoba. And I am not a unique case. This is as true for the majority of listeners in Canada, the United States and around the world, and Young's interest in old Spanish American and Native American cultures stretches that feeling of 'elsewhere' for many others. Sometimes, as is the case on *Zuma*, Young's topographies are both actual (Zuma Beach, north of Malibu, where Young was resident on Sea Level Drive in 1974) and lost in time (the demise of Moctezuma II's Aztec Empire in the early sixteenth century). And sometimes his meditation on place occurs between songs. For example, on two tracks written in the late 1960s, the apocalyptic 'city in the smog' of 'LA' contrasts with the bittersweet title track of *Everybody Knows This Is Nowhere*, on which the migrant singer dreams of being 'back home' where it is 'cool and breezy'. Distinct places can vanish into nowhere spaces and then re-emerge: Los Angeles is both real and nowhere in these two songs, while Young's childhood home, Omemee, is not actually 'a town in north Ontario', as the opening line of 'Helpless' describes it, but only 80 miles from the urban centre of Toronto. Young is not studiously historical or geographical in his research and at times he indulges in romanticism, but he is very often conscious of this, most obviously on his fantasy song

'Pocahontas' (1979), in which the musician-songwriter,
the Powhatan and iconic actor Marlon Brando (a champion
of Native American causes) sit around the campfire to reflect
on 'the astrodome and the first tepee'. Often bound up with
journeys and road travel, Young's geographies span the Americas
– past and present, north and south, rural and urban – in an
expansive manner that is rare among recording artists.

Travel between spaces, both literal and imaginative, is deeply
embedded in Young's songwriting and performances. It helps
to explain the sonic and lyrical contours of his music and the
experimental phases of his career over the 36 studio albums
he has released to date as a solo artist and with Crazy Horse,
together with his on–off membership of Buffalo Springfield
between 1966 and 1968 and of Crosby, Stills, Nash & Young since
he joined the trio in summer 1969. This is not to suggest that there
is a unified aesthetic that can be traced through the 50 years since
he performed his early songs 'Sugar Mountain' and 'Nowadays
Clancy Can't Even Sing' in the coffee houses of Yorkville,
Toronto. Rather, this book shows that the complex relationship
between space, place and time is at the heart of Young's music,
and that transition and travel underpin the songs of one of the
most significant recording and performing artists of the late
twentieth and early twenty-first centuries.

INTRODUCTION: TWISTED ROAD

The simplest way to become a musical enigma is to die young.
The 'what if' factor has preserved the legacy of Robert Johnson,
Hank Williams Sr, Jimi Hendrix, Janis Joplin, Jim Morrison and
Kurt Cobain like no other. False rumours of Paul McCartney's
death in a car crash in 1967 aged 25 (prompted by his rear-view
image on the back cover of *Sgt. Pepper's Lonely Hearts Club Band*)
added to the mystique of The Beatles during their most creative
phase. For a recording artist who doesn't burn out – as was the
case for five of these singers (the cause of Robert Johnson's death
remains a mystery) – preserving musical credibility over a long
span is trickier. It is risky to develop a signature sound early in
a musical career only to repeat it in the hope of capitalizing on
success. There is always the danger of the rust factor, as Neil
Young called it on his 1979 album *Rust Never Sleeps*, or of ending
up a 'park-bench' mutation, as he muses on 'Thrasher', where
musical vitality is traded in for a comfortable reputation. This
trajectory is not inevitable: Leonard Cohen, for example, has
moved only subtly from the elegiac sound he established in 1967
on *Songs of Leonard Cohen*. But other career musicians of that
generation, such as Neil Young, Bob Dylan and Joni Mitchell, have
frequently changed direction in order to revitalize their music.

Preserving privacy is part of this enigma, as Dylan has shown
by limiting personal interviews after facing press intrusion in the
mid-1960s. This is also true of Young, especially in the 1970s when
he became very distrustful of the media. But Young's enigma

stems also from his desire to retain tight control over his music, his restless songwriting and a defiant attitude towards the music industry. 'You gotta keep changing,' he told *Rolling Stone* in 1975, 'I'd rather keep changing and lose a lot of people along the way.'[1]

This enigmatic profile is encoded by conceptual artist Jeremy Deller in a poster that was first displayed at the Frieze Art Fair in London's Regent's Park in 2006 and included in Deller's 'Joy in People' exhibition at the Hayward Gallery, London, in 2012. The artwork has a simple design: a plain black background with five large words in white italicized capital letters centred one above the other, '*WHAT WOULD NEIL YOUNG DO?*' Mass-produced as a give-away poster, Deller's piece entices the viewer to improvise by developing the kind of oblique strategy that musician Brian Eno and painter Peter Schmidt pioneered in their lateral-thinking cards of the mid-1970s to encourage creative thinking and shake up daily routines. Deller claimed that he was inspired by Young's single-minded pursuit of his musical interests.[2] Based on the anecdote that Young's long-term manager Elliot Roberts would encourage him to consider 'what would Bob Dylan do?' before choosing a musical direction or embarking on a commercial venture, Deller's image hovers between a meditation on the art of the singer-songwriter and an empty commercial slogan.[3]

Young's enigma has also been fuelled by false rumours surrounding his death: it was reported that he had taken an overdose in Paris in October 1973; an NBC reporter mistakenly mentioned Neil Young when announcing the death of astronaut Neil Armstrong in August 2012; and he was one of a series of Internet hoaxes in November 2013.[4] Although he has mused about death (in his homage to Kurt Cobain on the title track of the 1994 album *Sleeps with Angels* and in the wake of long-term collaborator Ben Keith's death on 2010's 'Walk with Me') and has long been preoccupied with the passage of time (on 'Old Man' and 'Time Fades Away', for instance), a more interesting aspect

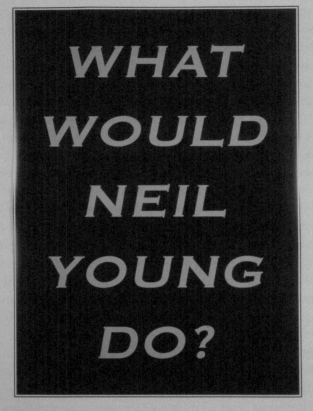

Jeremy Deller, *What Would Neil Young Do?*, poster, Frieze Art Fair, London, 2006.

of his enigma links to the theme of travel. This is not so surprising for someone who has been in the music business for 50 years, but it is helpful to think about Young's repertoire as a version of travelling music that links movement between geographical spaces to a fluid musical style.

Travel is much more important to Young than to most other musicians. He showed an early interest in cars and trains and he comments in his memoirs *Waging Heavy Peace* (2012) and *Special Deluxe* (2014) that travel quickly became a feature of his music and his life: 'I love travel. I got hooked on those trips when I was five, six years old. I think it was my dad. The highway bug. I've always loved it.'[5] Over his career Young has shifted styles and directions many times, moving from folk to rock, from country to electronica, and from grunge to noise, just as he has journeyed through the Americas, literally between Canada and the United States – most obviously in his one-way road trip from Toronto to Los Angeles in spring 1966 – and imaginatively into Central and South America. This notion of a 'poetics of energy' (to quote the title of William Echard's 2005 book[6]) means that Young is more interested in the activity of travel than reaching a fixed musical destination.

A good example of this restlessness is the short steel-guitar song 'Boxcar', first written in the late 1980s and revisited twenty years later for his album *Chrome Dreams II* (2007). The lyrics of 'Boxcar' stress Young's multiple identities as he transforms from a high-flying eagle into a low-lying snake and switches between racial identities. We might draw parallels between his chameleonic identity in the first verse of 'Boxcar' and the multiple personae of Bob Dylan in Todd Haynes's imaginative biopic *I'm Not There* released that same year, in which Dylan is played by six very different actors (one black, one female) with overlapping stories. *I'm Not There* suggests that Dylan underwent radical transformations, whereas Young's multiple identities in

'Boxcar' give way to a more stable image of a hobo travelling the freight train with no fixed destination. The lyrics of the earlier version reveal a restless rambler who leaves behind him a trail of broken relationships, but on the 2007 version he introduces varied topographies – coastline, desert line and mountain line (all are in danger of disappearing) – and 'the great spirit' who guides his journey.

Staying with this theme, in his memoir *Neil and Me* of 1984 Young's father, the renowned Toronto sportswriter Scott Young, titles one of the chapters 'Travelling Music'. The chapter focuses on the mid-1970s as an especially creative period for Neil, who was releasing acclaimed records at the same rate that he was shelving other album-length projects, most famously *Homegrown* in 1975 and *Chrome Dreams* in 1977. Scott Young documents his son's extensive travelling at this time, including a coastal bar tour of Northern California where Neil would reveal little about where he would play next, and the separate bus that kept him at arm's length from his old band mate Stephen Stills during their 1976 tour – only seven months after Young had made guest appearances at four of Stills's concerts.

This prompts Scott Young to think of his son as a musical version of Harry 'Rabbit' Angstrom, John Updike's restless small-town protagonist in the first two novels of his Rabbit quartet, *Rabbit, Run* and *Rabbit Redux*, in which Angstrom searches for a meaningful alternative to post-war suburbia. To be on the run is to define a life through movement and travel rather than in terms of accomplishment or success. Of course by the mid-1970s Neil Young was far removed from Angstrom's blue-collar background (his two most famous albums *After the Gold Rush* and *Harvest* made him a rich man) and locality (he bought a large ranch in La Honda near Santa Cruz in 1970), but his father detects an inner core that makes his son appear as if 'he was living out part of himself that perhaps he didn't want to lose in the rush of big events'.[7] This idea

Neil Young and Stephen Stills performing 'Only Love Can Break Your Heart' at the Capital Centre in Landover, Maryland, 1974.

of 'living out part of himself' chimes with the multiple identities Young has inhabited over his 50-year career: most obviously the 'Hollywood Indian' character he cultivated in his first Californian band Buffalo Springfield, but also the adoption of alter egos such as Bernard Shakey (the name he uses when directing films), Phil Perspective (as producer) and Joe Yankee (as percussionist), and his film characters Lionel Switch in *Human Highway* (1982) and Shakey Deal for an unrealized 1980s film project, *The Big Room*. Just as he moves between pseudonyms, his autobiographical voice drifts in and out of songs, often quite elusively. For example, on his 1989 track 'Crime in the City', a verse about Young's feelings of distance from his parental home shifts subtly into the voice of a fireman who is sent to prison for having a badass attitude. More obviously, it links to the enigma of a performer whose motivations are unpredictable and sometimes undecipherable. *Neil and Me* does not focus consistently on the theme of travel, but perceptively identifies movement as a central feature of Young's music.

We can see this feature most obviously in the title of the autobiographical track 'Twisted Road' from the 2012 album *Psychedelic Pill*, which also lent its name to Young's 2010 North American tour. The song introduces two signature themes of car travel and being away from home and proceeds at jaunty mid-tempo with a two-line refrain sung by Crazy Horse. Young is unashamedly nostalgic in identifying three musical sources from his early career: the rock poetry of Bob Dylan, the old-time West Coast hippie vibe of the Grateful Dead and the falsetto of Roy Orbison, whom he met after a 1962 concert in Winnipeg and whose 1960 single 'Only the Lonely' was the first 45-rpm record that Young owned.[8] 'Twisted Road' makes special mention of Dylan's 'Like a Rolling Stone', which Young first heard in summer 1965 before leaving Toronto for Los Angeles. In this pivotal song Dylan exchanges his acoustic guitar and topical folk lyrics for a clanging electric guitar and a new take on the American songbook. 'Twisted Road' has an easy familiarity: Dylan is referred to only via the title of 'Like a Rolling Stone'; the Dead play on the radio in the background; and Young feels an affinity with the Big O's delicate vocals and enigmatic image.[9]

Explicit musical referencing occurs occasionally in his songs. This is most obvious on the opening track of *Harvest Moon*, 'From Hank to Hendrix', the reference to The Beach Boys' melancholic 'Caroline No' on 'Long May You Run', and the mention of Willie Nelson and Chris Rock in the haunting 9/11 song 'No Wonder' from *Prairie Wind*. In 'Twisted Road' the music itself is the focus, not personalities. The magic of 'Like a Rolling Stone' inspires Young to 'take it home' and to give it a 'twist'. Rather than edging towards imitation, he emulates the spirit of Dylan's travelling music and the broader historical development of American roots music: in the words of Greil Marcus, 'how every phrase and image, every riff and chime, is always moving, state to state, decade to decade, never at home with whoever might claim it, always seeking a new body, a new song, a new voice'.[10]

The influences between Dylan and Young are not all one way.[11] The Minnesotan returned the compliment to the Canadian on his 1997 meditation on bucolic longing, 'Highlands', before visiting Young's teenage home in Winnipeg in 2008 and 2014. Dylan does not turn to pastoral or lyrical traditions for solace in 'Highlands', but to the amplified rock of his Canadian counterpart: he turns up the volume to listen to Young's music but finds that 'someone's always yelling turn it down'. This lyric not only emphasizes the pair's different paths in the 1980s and 1990s, but also acknowledges that Young's heavy sonic trajectory (especially his collaborations with Crazy Horse and Pearl Jam) is as much about wandering as the contemplative folk tradition that Dylan evokes in 'Highlands'. The solitary quest for meaning for Dylan late in his career is more spiritual than his topical folk songs of the early 1960s, but here it is Young's music that propels Dylan as he drifts 'from scene to scene'. This reference to 'drifting' is central to my reading of Young's music. Over 50 years he has drifted around questions of time, identity and place via a vast repertoire of songs that travel between intense alienation and feelings of being at ease with the world.

'Twisted Road' does not seek the profundity of 'Like a Rolling Stone', but the Dylan reference offers us a clue to what we can call Young's ragged or patchwork aesthetic. He often borrows riffs and motifs from other musicians and even from his own back catalogue, such as one of his first songs from 1964, 'I Wonder', which he revived as 'Don't Cry No Tears' a decade later.[12] Young has always sought to rearrange elements, either borrowed or recycled, into new combinations. We can find imitative songs elsewhere, most obviously in his fusion of the guitar styles of Randy Bachman and Hank Marvin in his early band The Squires,

or in his version of the raw guitar riff from The Rolling Stones'
breakthrough single '(I Can't Get No) Satisfaction' on Buffalo
Springfield's 'Mr Soul'. He self-consciously stole from the Stones'
1966 song 'Lady Jane' for the *Tonight's the Night* track 'Borrowed
Tune' and lifted the melody from Bert Jansch's 'Needle of Death'
for his 1974 slow-burner 'Ambulance Blues', before recording
Jansch's tune 40 years later on *A Letter Home*.[13] This tendency
echoes Dylan's technique of musical theft – or what Sean Wilentz
calls 'modern minstrelsy' – in his blending together of elements
from folk, blues and vaudeville.[14] Just as Dylan's songs can be
seen to combine 'tradition and defiance', so 'Like a Rolling Stone'
prompts Young to write a 'brand new song with familiar chords'.[15]

But it would be wrong to conclude that Young lurks in Dylan's
shadow. 'Twisted Road' is a fresh take on an old theme and also
a distinctive response to Dylan's question of how it feels 'to be
without a home'. We glimpse a mythical Robert Johnson figure
accompanied by 'the devil on a twisted road', but Young mostly
avoids the deeper questions about the dangers of success posed
by Dylan in 'Like a Rolling Stone' and instead offers an easy-going
answer: that he will 'let the good times roll' if he ever finds his
way home. Glimmers of media intrusion fade into a good-time
chorus in which mid-'60s music energizes the band, reflected in
the song's main verb phrases: walking, flying, singing and playing.

The previous track on *Psychedelic Pill*, 'Born in Ontario', is a
much more straightforwardly autobiographical song. It is also
a counterpoint to the brooding 'Hitchhiker' on the 2010 album
Le Noise, which retells Young's North American journey from
Ontario to Southern California and his retreat north up the Pacific
Coast to La Honda at the beginning of the 1970s. Given the
account in 'Hitchhiker' of drug-taking, break-ups and paranoia,
it is perhaps unsurprising that 'Twisted Road' was Young's initial
choice for an album title. But rather than recounting his personal
journey for a second time, 'Born in Ontario' revisits the cultural

nationalism that the Canadian government was encouraging for the centennial of 1967, the year after Neil Young and Joni Mitchell had left for the United States. Although Young felt uncomfortable with overt forms of nationalism early in his career, 40 years later there seems to be little ambivalence in his celebration of his Canadian roots. This is in contrast to a more ambiguous group of autobiographical songs released in the early 1970s that evoke his Canadian past: the yearning of 'Helpless', the defiance of 'Don't be Denied', and the nostalgia of 'Journey through the Past'. These tracks express both the 'rurality, directness and simplicity' of Canadian folk music and the displacement of a self-exiled Canadian.[16] In contrast, 'Born in Ontario' avoids nostalgia for the Canadian wilderness and small-town life in favour of a simple verse–chorus pattern and a relaxed, homely mood.

Another way of thinking about the relationship between the forms and themes of Young's music is in the activity of drifting. We can distinguish drifting from the more active rambling of blues music, in which the song's restless central character creates mayhem – usually crime or infidelity – everywhere he goes. The figures of the drifter and the rambler sometimes overlap (on Young's mesmerizing 1977 song 'Will to Love', for example), but the drifter is more resonant of the migration of many North American workers during the Great Depression. It is also in tune with a hippie sensibility of the late 1960s, as the drifter moves in and out of places with barely a trace and observes scenes casually before moving on.

It is tempting to identify this tendency in Young's early music, such as the impressionistic urban images of 'Don't Let it Bring You Down', the second track on side two of *After the Gold Rush*. The two verses of the song suggest a transition between early morning and night that debilitates the city's dwellers, symbolized by an old man who collapses under the weight of the urban environment. It also prompts the singer to think about how displacement, isolation and confusion often mark the modern city experience. These fragmentary insights do not come together in a panoramic vision. Instead, the archaic image of 'castles burning' in the chorus strains against the urban signs of roads, lorries, skyscrapers, alleys, red lights, sirens and gutters. Here the songwriter inhabits an indistinct space both inside and outside the city; he can see beyond the surface of things but is unable to leave behind this noisy environment. The 'turn' of the song ('just find someone who's turning') reveals a transformation of place and time rather than a full critique of urban life. Although the final line of the chorus ('and you will come around') suggests a source of comforting repose, it seems to be only temporary respite from urban drift.

In its resistance to fixed identities and policed spaces, Young's interest in drifting parallels a central idea of the French Situationists, a countercultural movement that promoted revolutionary ideas before its radical political agenda collapsed in the early 1970s. One of the key Situationist concepts is the *dérive*. This term suggests a self-conscious defiance of rules as the individual drifts around the city, relying on chance and intuition rather than following maps or being distracted by the urban spectacle. Young's politics have never been stable enough to claim that he systematically subverts the politics of space, but his music often suggests a reconfiguring of time and place. This could be compared with French sociologist Guy Debord's reflection on reality, outlined in the 1967 Situationist treatise *The Society of the Spectacle*. Debord believed that reality needs to be wrestled free from capitalist control before it can be saved from the 'shimmering diversions of the spectacle'.[17] He was concerned that the policing of urban spaces leads to a 'visible freezing of life', an inert condition that can only be overcome by self-initiated wandering.[18]

'Dérive' is one method for evading the expectations of urban planners, but so too is another Situationist concept, *détournement*.

Roughly translated, 'détournement' means the re-presentation (or 'turning') of an established idea that presents the individual with an opportunity to rescue meaning and agency from the spectacle. Détournement can involve wresting back control by defiantly stealing images or subverting habitual thought patterns by playing with language and expression – as do Eno and Schmidt's Oblique Strategies and the 2008 Drift Deck project, which encourages city wandering by means of puzzle-solving. The strong Marxist leaning of the Situationists cannot be easily applied to Young's music, but his status as a Canadian living in California during the exact phase of capitalism outlined in *Society of the Spectacle* is resonant, particularly as his songs explore techniques of drifting and turning.

This process of reconfiguring is best expressed in Young's famous statement on his most commercially successful early single, 'Heart of Gold', which went to Number One in both the u.s. and Canada in April 1972. Young claimed that this loosely autobiographical song, recounting his Californian journey from south to north, propelled his career to the 'middle of the road' before he deviated away into a less polished format for his 'ditch trilogy' of the mid-1970s: *Time Fades Away*, *On the Beach* and *Tonight's the Night*. In the liner notes of his 1977 compilation *Decade*, he comments that 'travelling' to the 'middle of the road . . . soon became a bore so I headed for the ditch. A rougher ride but I saw more interesting people there.' This comment links to the death of two of Young's friends from heroin overdoses (the second, Bruce Berry, features in the title track of *Tonight's the Night*), fallings out among the members of Crosby, Stills, Nash & Young (including an aborted recording of a reunion album written in Hawaii in 1973) and Young's increasing feelings of disaffection with the music industry. The contrast between 'track' and 'ditch' also features in another song on *Harvest*, 'Alabama', which abandons the metronomic beat of 'Heart of Gold' for a rawer sound in keeping with his ambivalence towards the South.

This suggests that roads are rarely straightforward for Young. As for the Beat writer Jack Kerouac, what lies off the road – or the act of 'driftin' along' without clear direction – means that journeys are always under way rather than moving purposefully towards a destination. This onward journey is encoded in a fascinating series of artworks by the Los Angeles-based artist Jenice Heo, one of which is included on the box design of *Neil Young Archives Vol. 1*. Heo's mixed-media assemblages are titled after thirteen of Young's songs, with an emphasis on the routes and vehicles that have carried him on his journeys.[19] The travelling theme is vividly portrayed in *Where is the Highway Tonight?*, which assembles an old speed limit sign, the front hood grille trim and operating manual of a Chevrolet, a Crow Indian belt and what Heo describes as 'an old found photograph, taken long ago from behind the front windshield of a moving car' revealing 'a patch of what appears to be a desert road or two-lane highway receding into the night' that evokes the spirit of Kerouac's *On the Road*.[20]

These planes of mobility, both geographical and musical, route through to Young's songwriting and are reprised in Gary Burden and Heo's travelling design for his 2014 album *Storytone* and its 2015 incarnation, *Mixed Pages of Storytone*, which reassembles the ten songs by interweaving orchestral and solo versions. On this theme, in an interview in 1990 Young claimed that 'I've written most of my best songs driving on a long journey scribbling lyrics on cigarette packets whilst steering', before commenting wryly on his musical travels: 'I've been running all my life. Where I'm going . . . Who the fuck knows? But that's not the point.'[21] This is illustrated in *Storytone*'s raw blues track 'I Want to Drive My Car', where he draws a parallel between driving 'further and further' and the need to find new musical fuel.

With these thoughts in mind, this book explores the importance of space and place in Young's music. The common trajectory of his songs is away from the city towards a re-engagement

with nature, such as on 'Thrasher', in which he chooses the lonely
open road over the 'park-bench mutations' that he fears some of
his industry friends have become. The idealized natural landscape
in the title track of *Harvest Moon* (1992) contrasts with corrupt
urban scenes pictured in the two opening songs of his previous
album *Freedom*, 'Rockin' in the Free World' and 'Crime in the
City'. He sometimes complicates the opposition between city
and country: on 'Don't Let it Bring You Down', for example, the
natural imagery of the 'blue moon' and 'river of sight' jar with
the urban experience. These spaces often lack sharp definition
but they are never empty; they can be full of unpredictable
transformations, but they rarely deter movement.[22] Sometimes
this movement is earthbound (walking or driving) and sometimes
an imaginative flight onwards (via birds or angels). They are often
uneasy journeys, though, and in danger of ending prematurely
or with the final destination receding beyond the horizon. This
unpredictability corresponds to Linda Ronstadt's description of
'strange jumps and shifts' in Young's brain: 'You never know if
he is going to explode or if he is going to be like a volcano or a
nice peaceful river.'[23]

Another way to think about the themes of drifting and flight
as components of Young's ragged aesthetic is via the image
of the bluebird. One of the most popular Buffalo Springfield
songs, 'Bluebird', is a three-part track written by Stephen Stills
in 1967. Described by Jimmy McDonough as a 'folk-pop-blues
confection', the bird is a metaphor for the free spirit of a loved
one who mesmerizes the songwriter with eyes that possess 'the
strangest colour blue'.[24] Taking flight does not occur in the first
lyrical section, but through Stills's virtuoso guitar playing in the
second part, which Young and Stills extended in live performances
with their duelling guitars 'pushing and pulling' the music 'to its

Jenice Heo, 'Where is the Highway Tonight?', oil on found objects, assemblage painting,
from the *Neil Young* series, 2010.

limit'.[25] In the studio version the third part of the song follows after a brief pause and trades the joy of the early section for sadness as the bluebird prepares to fly away.

Both Stills and Young returned to images of birds taking flight through their careers. We see this most obviously on 'Beautiful Bluebird', which Young first wrote in the mid-1980s for *Old Ways* and eventually included on *Chrome Dreams II*. Released 40 years after Stills had written 'Bluebird', Young's gentle song meditates on loss. Rather than the songwriter taking a journey through the past or drifting through a landscape, we see him driving his truck with no destination in view. He suddenly notices the iridescent bird 'dippin' and bobbin' in the sun' and decides to follow it down the road. This exact phrasing is also used for the opening of the more complex song 'No Wonder' two years earlier, a track that leads to an uncomfortable exploration of damage, betrayal and death. 'Beautiful Bluebird' steers away from deep emotions, but there is still an unfulfilled longing for a place of rest, even though she, like the singer, appears to have no fixed horizon. Young reaches for a similar metaphor to Stills when the song turns from a musing on home to reflect on a lost love that has flown away. Despite the large population of North American bluebirds, the brilliant blue suggests an exceptional love which cannot be captured and inspires movement onwards. The tight lyrical focus of 'Beautiful Bluebird' prevents it from drifting far off track, but it nevertheless suggests a movement that cuts across space and time.

There are further elements here to which I will return – the importance of colour and the shifting status of home – but we can see in Young's rewriting of Stills's 'Bluebird' a revival of one of Buffalo Springfield's most iconic songs in a more lyrical mode. This could be seen as a form of re-presentation that returns us to Debord's theory of détournement. In this way, Young's songs often move both backwards and forwards in an attempt to find 'genuine life' (as Debord calls it) within everyday modes of expression that might otherwise lead to the 'paralysis of history and memory'.[26] More simply, his music can be seen as an ongoing journey to redefine ideas of freedom, agency and identity within a shifting capitalist system, to which the musical industry was becoming increasingly bound during the 1970s.

Young rarely resorts to the poetry of Dylan's most expressive phase. Instead, by working with colloquial language and impressionistic images he pushes the listener to reconsider the clichés of popular music. This aspect of his writing can be traced back to the Canadian folk music of his early years, but also links to Debord's argument that 'common language' is often sacrificed within the pseudo-reality of urban life.[27] That is not to say that Young does not want listeners to immerse themselves, particularly in his extended songs with Crazy Horse, but this is balanced by his search for common language that can anchor moments of visionary insight before they vanish or become obscured by the sheen of late capitalism. We see this tension in the dazzling iridescence of the bluebird that disturbs the singer momentarily, before he is led on by the more commonplace lyric 'dippin' and bobbin' in the sun'.

We will see later the importance of dream and vision for some of Young's most significant songs. This interest links to his exposure to West Coast psychedelic music and his engagement with Native American cultural practices, particularly the 'vision quest' which expands reality via an immersive experience that opens up past and future. Young's interest in dreaming is also there in the imaginative arc of his Canadian songs 'Helpless' and 'Journey through the Past' and is beautifully conveyed in a painting by former student Laura Clark on the wall of Kelvin High School in Winnipeg. In this painting the troubadour musician reclines on a couch with a view of bright blue sky and the yellow Manitoban plains through the window, offering a vista of his Canadian past and a portal into the future.

I will return to five elements of this ragged aesthetic –
drifting, turning, dreams, language and musical form – via the
themes of travel and movement. The six chapters also sketch
out the two musical modes for which Young is best known: the
autobiographical acoustic songs of the late 1960s and 1970s usually
played percussively on acoustic guitar or piano, and the electric
guitar tracks with Crazy Horse. The first mode is characterized by
lyrical poise and the second is 'funkier, simpler, more down to the
roots'.[28] In addition, I am interested in Young's broader cultural
production. This includes his self-directed films *Journey through
the Past* (1972) and *Human Highway* (1982), his collaborations with
directors Jim Jarmusch and Jonathan Demme, and his memoirs,
Waging Heavy Peace (2012) and *Special Deluxe* (2014), the last of
which closes with an account of his transcontinental road trip in
LincVolt, his converted fuel-efficient 1959 Lincoln Continental.[29]

The first four chapters are organized chronologically. The
opening chapter traces Young's roots in Canadian music and his
reflections on growing up, before the book moves on to discuss
his journey from Toronto to Los Angeles and his prominent role
in the Laurel Canyon scene. Chapter Three shifts focus to assess

Laura Clark's painting of Neil Young, 2005, displayed on the wall at Kelvin High School,
River Heights, Winnipeg.

Young's attempts to confront and reconfigure the American South, just as the South was undergoing its own sociological and musical transitions. In chapter Four I return to California to see how the San Francisco Bay Area offers a direct contrast to the urban experience of Los Angeles. This is embodied in Young's move to La Honda in 1970 and emerges periodically in his music, most prominently in his eco-concept album *Greendale* (2003).

The final chapters deal with space and place in a more fluid way. The fifth chapter looks at his interest in dream imagery and mythic retelling via a number of extended tracks written between 1968 and 1977 – 'Broken Arrow', 'Country Girl (Medley)', 'Cortez the Killer', 'Like a Hurricane' and 'Pocahontas' – while the final chapter considers how his sonic experiments on albums such as *Trans* and *Arc/Weld* explore the music of travelling. The conclusion maintains the focus on journeys in the shape of the CSNY track 'Human Highway', but it also discusses Young's more politicized activities that have sometimes motivated his musical projects. Although Neil Young has been claimed as both an innovator and a traditionalist, this book shows that his role as a musical traveller on a twisted road transcends easy categorization.

The entranceway of Massey Hall, Toronto, the venue of two of Young's defining performances, on 19 January 1971.

1 MANITOBA AND ONTARIO

Neil Young arrived in Los Angeles on 1 April 1966 in a road-weary black Pontiac hearse. Affectionately named Mort II, this second hearse followed the demise of Mort, his '48 Buick Roadmaster, when its transmission failed on a road trip the previous summer. That journey ended near Blind River, Ontario – later immortalized in the lyrics of 'Long May You Run' – and included Bob Clark, the new drummer of Young's first serious band The Squires.[1] The four-piece group had first formed at Kelvin High School in the prairie city of Winnipeg in early 1963 and swiftly developed a strong instrumental style, making them one of the busiest acts to play in the city's community clubs and coffee houses. Sensing broader opportunities further afield, in autumn 1964 The Squires began playing in the fur-trading town of Fort William, now part of Thunder Bay, on the western shore of Lake Superior. For ten months they had a good run in Fort William as the house band at The Flamingo Club, returning periodically to play in Winnipeg. But the end of Mort, their makeshift tour bus, prompted them to embark on another journey, 800 miles to the southeast.

This move to Toronto in summer 1965 proved less successful. There the band renamed themselves Four to Go after finding a local group with a similar name, but they struggled to find work in the coffee houses and bars of bohemian Yorkville at the centre of Toronto's music scene.[2] Young picked up some solo acoustic

gigs at the Yorkville venues the New Gate of Cleve and the
Riverboat but, frustrated at being in an unknown band, he set his
sights elsewhere. After his next group The Mynah Birds split in
February 1966, when American singer Ricky James Matthews was
busted for avoiding the draft (during the recording of the band's
debut album in Detroit), Young's desire to travel heightened.
'I knew I had to leave Canada', he later said, 'and the sounds I was
hearing and the sounds I liked were coming from California.
I knew if I went down there I could take a shot at making it.'[3]

Young often talks decisively about his reasons for leaving
Canada, but the musical impetus to do so was complex. A defining
moment in his development as a singer-songwriter was seeing
Bob Dylan on the Canadian TV show *Quest* in 1964, especially
because Dylan's rasping voice contrasted starkly with the slick
vocal arrangements of the typical band. Dylan was not just a
distant icon: he twice visited Toronto in 1965 to rehearse with
The Hawks in September (they renamed themselves The Band
after touring with Dylan in 1966) and to play at Massey Hall in
November. Young did not see him live on either occasion, but the
Minnesotan's electric folk had a lasting effect. An early indication
of this is The Squires' performance of Dylan's 'Just Like Tom
Thumb's Blues' in Killington, Vermont in October 1965. This
travelling song about a displaced northerner who encounters
corruption and sickness in Mexico set a travelling tone for the
callow Canadian musician, and he chose to reprise the track for
his two-song set at Dylan's 30th Anniversary Concert in 1992.[4]

Young's musical sensibility was honed by a number of
visiting American acts that played at the cluster of cafés and
bars in Yorkville, such as the Southern blues duo Sonny Terry
and Brownie McGhee, but of equal importance was his contact
with Canadian musicians. These included Joni Mitchell (they
first met when Young took a trip to Winnipeg in December 1965;
she lived in Detroit during her short-lived marriage and she left

for New York around the time he went to California); Gordon Lightfoot (he had spent fourteen months in Los Angeles as a jazz student in the late 1950s and became the headline act at the 120-seater Riverboat Coffee House when it opened in 1965); and Ian and Sylvia Tyson (the pair left Toronto for New York in 1962 and had released four albums by the time Young arrived in Yorkville, including *Early Morning Rain*, named after Lightfoot's 1964 song). Although Lightfoot returned to Canada in 1960 after an uninspiring time in Los Angeles, these musical journeys suggest that there were limited opportunities in Toronto, despite the convergence of talent on Yorkville, the Canadian version of Greenwich Village.

The most important encounter for shaping Young's travel plans was his meeting with Texas-born Stephen Stills, who performed with The Company (a spin-off from Stills's first band, the Au Go-Go Singers) at the Fourth Dimension Club in Fort William in April 1965. Stills had travelled extensively as a child and teenager and absorbed a number of musical influences, including folk and blues from the Deep South and Latin American rhythms from spells in Costa Rica and Panama. This version of travelling music proved exciting for the twenty-year-old Canadian. After sharing the bill at The Flamingo Club, Young and Stills expressed their admiration for each other's musical versatility. Stills thought Young's songwriting was primitive, but he later noted that he was 'doing the same thing I wanted to do . . . playing folk music with an electric guitar. And Neil had such an interesting, intense attitude.'[5] The pair agreed to play together in the future and planned to meet in Manhattan, but it took a year before they found each other again in Los Angeles.[6]

We might see Young's trip to California in March 1966 as a punctuation mark dividing his Canadian and American years. But his musical development was in transit from an early age, with Canada functioning both as a horizon and a point of departure, as it did when the Young family travelled by car for extended breaks in the early 1950s from cold Omemee, Ontario, to tropical New Smyrna Beach, Florida, to aid Neil's recuperation from polio.[7] It is significant that two tracks on The Squires' only recorded single of November 1963, 'The Sultan' and 'Aurora', hint at exotic places, particularly as 'The Sultan' opens and closes with a clashing gong and 'aurora' is intoned mysteriously at the end of the song.[8] Reflecting the tight instrumental arrangements of The Shadows, The Ventures and The Fireballs, the mixture of skiffle rhythms, duelling guitars and surf pop brought a feeling of elsewhere to the long winters of Manitoba.

Another important track in Young's early repertoire was the contemporary folk song 'High Flying Bird', written by West Virginian Billy Edd Wheeler. The Squires performed the song in 1964 and it even became the band's name briefly. A track recorded by Stephen Stills with the Au Go-Go Singers, 'High Flying Bird', focuses on the desire to fly free and the reality of being rooted to the ground. The song proved very popular – it was recorded by Jefferson Airplane in 1966 and performed by Richie Havens during his opening act at the Woodstock Festival – and Young chose to revive The Squires' version nearly 50 years later for his *Americana* album. On this 2012 recording his anguished voice conveys the coal miner's despair as he looks up longingly at the soaring bird. However, the driving electric guitars suggest that the bird's powerful wing beat at least offers some hope for the singer's suffering. There is no explicit geographical reference, but the lyrics suggest that the rise and fall of the sun is accompanied by what one might imagine to be the bird's migratory flight southwards. The imagery of 'High Flying Bird' echoes through a number of Young's early compositions: in the melancholic Buffalo Springfield song 'Expecting to Fly', for example, the singer stumbles to the ground as his departing love readies herself for flight. This is not dissimilar to Dylan's 'Just Like Tom Thumb's

Blues', where moving forward feels like 'drifting backward', but in Young's early songs this is often expressed via shifting time signatures and the tension between an urge to take flight and frustrating inertia.[9]

His early interest in Elvis Presley, Bob Dylan, The Shadows and The Beatles did not mean that Young's influences were only from the U.S. and UK. The Canadian folk revival was also an important factor in his musical development and he would have been aware of the *Folk Songs of Canada* collection published by folklorist Edith Fowke in 1954 (she had her own CBC radio show, *Folk Sounds*, from 1963), the Folkways album *Folk Songs of Ontario* (1958) and the first Mariposa Folk Festival, held in Orillia, Ontario, in August 1961, which included many Yorkville bands and featured Ian & Sylvia as the headline act. More specifically, some of Young's earliest Canadian recordings were reworked for Buffalo Springfield; the lead singer of Winnipeg band The Guess Who, Randy Bachman, was a lasting influence on his guitar style; and he cited Ian & Sylvia's migration ballad 'Four Strong Winds' as his favourite folk song, rerecording it for his *Comes a Time* album.

Canadian topographies and themes continued to inflect Young's songs up to his 2012 album *Psychedelic Pill* – including the plainest statement of his national and regional origins in 'Born in Ontario' – and in his return to the Canada of his past in Jonathan Demme's 2011 film *Neil Young Journeys*. Young has described this periodic return to his early years as 'flashes of things in my past . . . images here and there that are about Canada'.[10] Just as Ernest Hemingway claimed that he could not write about his home state of Michigan until he was far away in Europe, Young had neither the perspective nor the technique to link together these 'flashes' and 'images' until he set out on his defining journey in early 1966.[11]

In his book *Neil Young: Don't Be Denied* (1993), a study of Young's early musical experiences, John Einarson claims that Young never left Canada behind and that movement and displacement marked his formative years in Ontario and Manitoba. This was especially true of 1960. Following the separation of his parents, Scott and Edna Young, the fourteen-year-old Neil travelled with his mother (known as Rassy) to start a new life in her home town of Winnipeg. Young's journey to California in 1966 was thus not his only life-defining road trip. His early years were full of moving: the 80-mile trip from the small town of Omemee (then with a population of 750) to the metropolis of Toronto (population 1.5 million); the recuperative vacations to Florida; the long trip northwest from Toronto to Winnipeg; then 80 miles east from the prairie city to the emerging music scene of Fort William; and a further 500 miles to Toronto for eight months, before the longer continental journey south and west. Young's interest in geography emerged subtly in his formative years in favour of a mode of introspective songwriting that quickly outgrew the tight style of The Squires, even though he tried to expand their repertoire with idiosyncratic versions of the folk standards 'Oh! Susanna' and 'Tom Dooley'.

The theme of childhood and growing up was a frequent subject of Young's early lyrics and carried over into the music he composed during his four years in Los Angeles. We can locate this most obviously in his alto vocal style which, in its 'hesitant, whiny, masculine and feminine' timbre (as Rickie Lee Jones describes it), evokes the uncomfortable transition between childhood and adulthood, while conveying 'all the sadness and unresolved' angst of being a teenager.[12] Childhood is a state of mind for Young, sometimes bewildering and uncomfortable and at other times a place of surprise and wonder. This is conveyed in the Ontario chapter of *Waging Heavy Peace*, in which Young moves from describing the L-shaped layout of his train set in his bedroom in Omemee to his medical treatment when he contracted polio at age six in 1951.[13] This does not mean that childhood could not be happy and exuberant. We see such a mood expressed in his foreword to a book of Canadian rural photography, *Down Home* (1997), in which Young remembers hunting turtles, fishing for perch and admiring colourful pansies as a child in a local Omemee store.[14]

Musically, this spirit is best expressed in his 1968 song 'I Am a Child'. This Buffalo Springfield track is often seen as a retort to Richie Furay's 'A Child's Claim to Fame', which appears to accuse Young of indulging in 'make believe'. 'I Am a Child' suggests that childhood contains hidden comforts and even a stubborn resilience in the face of adult pressures. But Young's reflections on childhood are typically marked by alienation. Even the protective space of 'I Am a Child' shifts from the comforting blue of the sky and sea to the troubling question 'what is the color when black is burned?' This arresting image darkens the song and links to Young's first recorded vocal track with Buffalo Springfield, 'Burned', which conveys the discomfort of being thrust into the public limelight. Childhood is rarely a bounded space for Young and it is often characterized by awkward transition and a melancholic sense of time passing – a mood to which he returned in his sentimental mid-1980s track 'My Boy', on which he wonders why his son Zeke's childhood is vanishing so rapidly.

His best-known song about growing up, 'Sugar Mountain', was written as he approached his nineteenth birthday while staying in Victoria Hotel in Fort William, but he rarely performed it at the time as it was not a good fit for The Squires. The song treats both childhood and adulthood as psychological states of displacement, leading a 1970 reviewer to describe it as 'five and a half minutes of Young and his guitar weeping away acoustically'.[15] His folky guitar style highlights a longing to return to a lost place that the singer feels he is forced to leave prematurely. The central image of 'Sugar Mountain' is simultaneously appealing and cloying: both a snowy landscape and a fairground attraction, signalled by the references to barkers, candy floss and colourful balloons. The appearance of a 'girl just down the aisle' who passes the singer a secret message and the excitement of smoking for the first time convey the joys of growing up, but also indicate that he cannot rediscover the juvenile space for which he longs. The song travels from the protective parental image of the first verse to the leave-taking in the final verse when the singer announces that he needs to be alone. In this way 'Sugar Mountain' is typical of Young's autobiographical style. It feels intensely personal, but its insistent second-person address ('You can't be twenty' living on Sugar Mountain) speaks to post-pubescent worries about growing up. Tellingly, his vocal inflection means that, without the lyrics to hand, it is hard to work out if he sings 'can't' or 'can', suggesting that one can indulge in childhood delights for a while longer.

This ambivalence is reflected in another of Young's early songs, which was to become half of Buffalo Springfield's first double A-side. The recorded version of 'Nowadays Clancy Can't Even Sing' is sung melodically by Richie Furay, whom Young had first met in Manhattan in October 1965 while trying to locate the whereabouts of Stephen Stills, around the time of an unsuccessful demo of seven songs at Elektra Records. Furay's vocal on 'Clancy' possesses a lilting poignancy, but Young's version, which he performed solo in Toronto and occasionally after Buffalo Springfield split, is more melancholic. Jimmy McDonough likens the song's composition to writer William S. Burroughs's and film-maker Nicholas Roeg's cut-up methods – in which logical connections between words, ideas and images are stretched – but he argues that Young's expression is more 'powerfully primitive' and conveys a 'naive, almost preposterous beauty'.[16] Tracing the logic in the sequence of images in 'Clancy' is frustrating. The song does not follow a regular pattern of growing up and it is not as time-bound as Joni Mitchell's 'The Circle Game', written in response to 'Sugar Mountain' and in which the child ages with each new verse. Nonetheless, there is an emotional arc to 'Clancy', as the indignant surprise of the first line – 'Hey, who's that stompin' all over my face?' – blends with Young's melancholic vocals. Although the first word of the title, 'Nowadays', suggests dislocation from the past, there is no yearning for a day when Clancy would or could sing.

The song is often associated with Neil's Winnipeg classmate Ross 'Clancy' Smith, who did not fit in with any friendship groups, perhaps because he was considered an outsider as a Canadian Jew or because of his multiple sclerosis: a subject that foreshadows Young's longstanding interest in conditions that affect both body and mind, including his own epilepsy (which plagued him in Los Angeles), his sons Zeke's and Ben's cerebral palsy, and his father's Alzheimer's disease. The song is a good example of Young's desire to rework complex life experiences into a troubling meditation on identity: Young saw Clancy as a 'strange cat' and respected him for his differences, but other kids just saw him as a 'weirdo'.[17]

'Clancy' is structured around a series of questions through which the singer attempts to identify an unnamed figure whose actions are linked to violation and annoyance in the first verse, obsession and play-acting in the second, and potential psychosis in the final verse. There is ultimately no answer to the questions of who is acting in this way, and these might well be different figures as one image blurs and dissolves into the next. The first verse floats free of a distinct space, while later spaces are enclosed and entrapping. Being 'down on the floor' and looking through the floorboard cracks enables him to see more clearly than a privileged vantage point would, but this is the strung-out perspective of a sleep-deprived singer who yearns for a better emotional place where he would not be 'so damn wrong'. This feeling of persecution intensifies to such a degree that the singer turns recrimination initially levelled at the persecuting figure who stomps on his face in on himself by the end.

'Clancy' is not a song about geographical travel in an external sense and there is no specific reflection on Canada, except for the possible classroom source. But it is full of uncomfortable transformations, descending into and beyond the self to a place where he sees eyes staring back at him. This shift into a surrealist inner landscape is in direct contrast to the folk repertoire of Gordon Lightfoot, whose view of the Canadian landscape is evoked in more specific detail than Young's 'flashes' and 'images'. Psychological states in Lightfoot's songs are usually linked to natural imagery, such as the brooding 'The Way I Feel' and the travelling song 'Crossroads', two tracks on Lightfoot's second album of 1967 in which the renewing power of nature offers solace from loneliness. Lightfoot's 'Song for a Winter's Night', 'Crossroads' and the nationalistic 'Canadian Railroad Trilogy' (a six-minute epic commissioned to launch the centennial year) are panoramic in their scope. These tracks retain a stable sense of regional identity and place, even as they explore 'the psychology of open spaces that makes up the mood of life in the biggest part of Canada', as described on the back cover of his debut album.[18] Lightfoot's role as national balladeer, particularly in the centennial year, was underlined by the fact that he remained within the folk fraternity rather than following Dylan down the road to electric folk. He was a great admirer of Dylan and his breakthrough song 'Early Morning Rain' took inspiration from Dylan's image of a lonesome traveller.[19] But when the two played at the Newport Folk Festival in July 1965, the Minnesotan's musical bravado far surpassed the Ontarian's earnest folk repertoire. In contrast to Lightfoot, and in common with Dylan, Young's songs rarely retain stable borders between psychology and environment or between distinct musical forms, as if he is subtly questioning what Lightfoot took to be an essential quality of the Canadian national character.

Three songs that best reflect Young's unstable yet resilient Canadian identity are the yearning 'Helpless', the nostalgic 'Journey through the Past' and the defiant 'Don't be Denied'.

All three tracks were written between 1969 and 1973 and express Young's 'haunting anxiety about what it meant to be nationalistic'.[20] Even though he returned to play at the Riverboat in February 1969 and Massey Hall in January 1971, by then he was suitably far away from Canada to be able to gain some perspective, and he uses the locations of Omemee and Winnipeg to ground the songs in moments from his early life.

'Helpless' is one of the most delicate renditions of his career. Played gently on three chords, ironically he auditioned with the song when Crosby, Stills & Nash were looking for extra guitar power. Recorded at 4 a.m., 'when everyone got tired enough to play at my speed' (as Young commented in the sleeve notes to *Decade*), the 'flashes of things' from the past are conveyed through a series of impressions in which internal and external landscapes blend. The beginning of the song is mythical ('There is a town in north Ontario'), but it soon settles into autobiographical mode where Young evokes the changes that he underwent there. Thereafter the lyrics mingle reflection, shadows, colours and movement, punctuated by the soulful single-word chorus on which Crosby and Nash harmonize. Young was to take the colour tones of 'Helpless' (the 'blue, blue windows' and the 'yellow moon on the rise') through to his *On the Beach* album, but here blues and yellows blend intriguingly into watercolour memories and a melancholic image of taking flight. Despite its simplicity, 'Helpless' conveys a nuanced emotion that McDonough describes as 'primordial, aching, trancelike'.[21] It illustrates the instability between psychological states and the natural world that marks his Canadian songs, revealing an umbilical connection to his homeland despite his migration. The ambivalence continues into the chorus: it is not clear what causes the helplessness or whether it is debilitating (perhaps linked to his childhood polio) or rejuvenating (an ability to feel strongly).

Young explores a similar sentiment on the piano ballad 'Journey through the Past', written around the same time as

'Helpless', in which his new ranch in La Honda, California becomes a time capsule to transport him into the past. Young admitted that he wrote 'Journey through the Past' on the road, but it is more stable than 'Helpless' and contrasts with the domestic song 'Time Fades Away' on the same album that recounts the teenage Neil's tense relationship with his mother. Inclement weather lends 'Journey through the Past' a different mood to 'Helpless', making him long for his lost love. He explores a similar wintry mood in 'Winterlong', later released on *Decade*. This song title was perhaps inspired by the seasonal deep freeze of Winnipeg, but the 'winter rain' of 'Journey through the Past' is closer to the stasis of Young's flying songs than to the dreamlike yearning of 'Winterlong'. Premiered at Massey Hall, the piano in 'Journey through the Past' reaches a crescendo in the second verse when he name-checks Canada and introduces the travelling comradeship of a fiddler and drummer.[22] Much simpler than Joni Mitchell's 'The Fiddle and the Drum' from her 1969 album *Clouds* (Mitchell pictures a war-mongering nation that has traded the folk fiddle for the military drum), Young's song suggests that the fiddler and the drummer would benefit from staying with each other. This mutual need is reinforced as the piano strengthens in the third verse in a moment of coming together, where journeys align rather than diverge.

In contrast to the waltz-like melancholy of 'Helpless' and the nostalgic piano strains of 'Journey through the Past', 'Don't be Denied' is a more straightforward travelling song. Played on electric guitar with a strong drum beat, it is delivered with a degree of anguish in the aftermath of Crazy Horse guitarist Danny Whitten's heroin overdose. The song recounts Young's journey from Toronto to Winnipeg after Neil's father left home, his experience of bullying in school and the formation of The Squires. Despite what one review calls 'the private trials of a rather delicate kid in a rugged land', the repetition of the song's title in the chorus suggests resilience in the face of dislocation.[23] This strength is carried into the middle section when the location shifts south to Young's two years playing gigs with Buffalo Springfield on Sunset Strip. The second half of the song focuses on the industry pressures of suddenly being a member of a successful band and Young's discomfort with the limelight. 'Don't be Denied' is structurally loose enough to avoid implying that Canada possesses an authenticity that a commercialized Los Angeles lacks, but the sequence of verses works to link together Young's travels and to lend Whitten's untimely death extra poignancy.

Young's thawing relation to Canada can be seen in the opening of his long 1974 track 'Ambulance Blues', on which he mourns the demise of the coffee houses that provided the stage for the 'old folky days' of the Yorkville scene (although the Riverboat did not close until 1978). This reconnection with the geography of his past is reflected in his recording of 'Four Strong Winds' for the *Comes a Time* album, released fifteen years after the original by Ian & Sylvia. Often dubbed Canada's 'unofficial national anthem', 'Four Strong Winds' explores the topic of 'leaving things behind' (a theme to which Young has said that he closely relates), as the migrant travels west to Alberta in the hope of finding a sense of renewal that his current relationship lacks.[24] There is only one direct reference to Canadian geography, in the mention of the province of Alberta, the folk tradition of which was being documented in detail for the first time in the late 1970s in the pages of the *Canadian Folk Music Journal*.[25] For Young, who first heard the song as a teenager gigging with his band at the picturesque Falcon Lake in southeast Manitoba, Alberta is a symbol both of the Canadian north and the North American west, where the sweeping majesty of nature compensates for a relationship that is unlikely to rekindle. The song's yearning is conveyed as much by Nicolette Larson's backing vocal as Young's

gentle delivery on *Comes a Time*. But the emphasis is more
powerfully on location and seasonal change than the ambivalence
the singer feels for the loved one he leaves behind. This emphasis
can be heard especially in his performance during the encore at
the Ryman Auditorium in Nashville in April 2005, played with
a full country band, with Pegi Young and Emmylou Harris on
backing vocals, as captured in the *Heart of Gold* film.

When Young returned to Canada later in his career it was
often as a vehicle to work through his relationship with his
parents. The central image of 'Four Strong Winds' offers a
more basic answer to the probing questions that Dylan poses in
'Blowin' in the Wind': the solution for Young is a reconnection to
the land and seasonal change. However, when he evokes similar
imagery on his *Prairie Wind* album it has a much darker tone.
Linked closely to Scott Young's death from Alzheimer's in 2005,
but also relating to his own neurological complications (which
led to surgery for an aneurysm the following year), the cover of
Prairie Wind, designed by Gary Burden and Jenice Heo, presents
a flat agrarian landscape in sepia colour tones. Two distant
homesteads can be glimpsed on the horizon to the middle left,
while a large sheet billowing in the wind in the right foreground
creates the optical illusion of a bird's wing or a white cliff. It is
difficult to locate the scene, suggesting that it could as easily be
the flat prairies of Nebraska or Minnesota as those of Manitoba
or eastern Alberta. That there are no figures in this landscape
suggests that the prairie wind is an inhuman force that strips away
identity. It is only when the artwork is folded out to show a young
woman with a wicker basket hanging out the washing that the
fuller image is revealed, as if the landscape on the front cover
cannot expose the whole picture.

There is something at once nostalgic and unsettling about
the cover image of *Prairie Wind*, taking its inspiration from the
vast prairies in which identity can fade into a feeling of 'essential

Young and friends playing against a prairie backdrop at the Ryman Auditorium, Nashville, in April 2005; still from *Neil Young: Heart of Gold* (dir. Jonathan Demme, 2005).

helplessness', as Carol Shields's character Daisy Goodwin muses in her 1993 novel *The Stone Diaries*.[26] This tone carries through into the album's long title track, where the prairie wind blows uncomfortably through the singer's head, emphasized by the persistent female vocals of the chorus. The struggle to remember the past and to piece together a coherent narrative of family and home centres on the image of Young's father 'before too much time took away his head'. The location here is not the singer's past, but Cypress River in Southern Manitoba, where Scott Young was born in 1918. The lyrics focus on the empty landscape and the struggle to remember clearly in the face of worsening dementia. In this indistinct world even natural and spiritual renewal might prove to be a 'mirage' when the vision of a dreamlike journey illuminated by the magical Northern Lights is brought back to earth with the jarring image of a 'new car' parked in an 'old garage'.

The title track, 'Prairie Wind', then, returns to one of Young's early themes: the tension between the desire to travel or fly and the inability to do so, where the landscape becomes a projection of a mind struggling to cling to meaningful memories. Rather than drifting back to the memory of pleasant times, the prairie wind is a forceful elemental energy that reminds us of the fragility of human life. However, there are consolations in the face of helplessness. The philosophical and personal discomfort of 'Prairie Wind' is tempered by another, more joyful album track, 'Far from Home'. This nostalgic song pictures Young's father, uncle and cousins on the porch singing 'bury me out on the prairie', a line deriving from the traditional folk ballad 'The Cowboy's Lament', but here turned into a celebration of his Canadian family.[27]

When it came for Young to reflect on his mother's death nine years later in the spoken introduction to *A Letter Home* (2014), he did so in a semi-humorous mood. He begins the album by saying hello to his mother from beyond the grave (she died in 1990) and expressing his wish that she and his father will finally settle their differences. This provides another time capsule, returning the listener to the folk tunes that inspired the young singer in the 1960s, including two tracks by Lightfoot and one by Dylan. Young expressed his intention to write a letter to all his friends on *Harvest Moon*, but it took him more than twenty years to do so. The twelve acoustic songs on *A Letter Home* cover a broad span of emotions, but with a special emphasis on travel. This invitation to journey through time and space is mirrored by his decision to record the songs in a 1940s Voice-O-Graph booth, which reminds him of a Seabreeze phonograph that his mother bought when he was a teenager.[28]

One of the standout tracks on *A Letter Home* is the delicate rendition of Bruce Springsteen's 1985 song 'My Hometown'. The

Neil Young at the Honour the Treaties Tour press conference, Calgary, 19 January 2014.

song links the geographies of Young's childhood in Omemee, Toronto and Winnipeg to his environmentalist causes, which took him back to Alberta in early 2014 to protest the polluting effects of the Fort McMurray oil sands on the land of the local Athabasca Chipewyan First Nations tribe.[29] Young turns Springsteen's New Jersey song into a more generalized response to Canada, pivoting on the shift of pronoun from 'my hometown' to 'your hometown' in the chorus. The song begins with a nostalgic return to childhood and memories of the singer's father, before shifting in the second verse to focus on racial hatred in the 1960s and economic depression in the 1970s Rust Belt. This gloom convinces the singer in the final verse to decide that his family should leave town and head south.

The autobiographical links for Young are limited to the southerly direction of travel, but the final image of 'My Hometown' is of the singer and his son sitting in his truck for one last look at the town before they leave. This returns us to the ambivalent images of travel and inertia that haunt Young's mid-1960s songs. But it is the act of letter-writing – presented here as a personalized collection of songs dedicated to his mother – that alleviates the melancholy of Dylan's take on the American songbook, 'I Was Young When I Left Home', where the singer finds himself in a wretched state of permanent exile because he 'never wrote a letter to my home'.[30]

2 LOS ANGELES

Los Angeles had been on Neil Young's mind ever since meeting Stephen Stills in Thunder Bay in April 1965 and his plans started to take shape that winter when he discovered that Stills had moved to California. By the following spring he was ready for change after a frustrating eight months in Toronto had convinced him that he should seek his musical future in the Golden State. Leaving Toronto on a wintry late March day, six Canadian travellers entered the United States in Young's latest hearse, Mort II, by the Lake Superior crossing of Sault Ste Marie, armed with the story that they were visiting Neil's mother in Winnipeg and that the drive south of the Great Lakes was much quicker. The quiet border crossing at night was straightforward. From there the route went south through Wisconsin, Illinois and Missouri, then veered southwest via Oklahoma and west through North Texas and New Mexico. Young did most of the 3,300-mile drive himself because he was worried that Mort II would develop a similar transmission fault to its predecessor. Lack of sleep, a diet of junk food and a mixture of amphetamines and downers to keep him going meant that the ride was physically and mentally taxing on Young. By the time the group arrived in Albuquerque, three-quarters of the way into the journey, they were fractious and had lost their early enthusiasm.

Young revisited this somnolent mood seven years later on the dreamlike track 'Albuquerque' for the *Tonight's the Night* album, written late at night after a tequila session. It conveys the loneliness and sleeplessness of a driver who finds himself in a world of his own despite the presence of others. The lyrics begin with a reflection on the distance to the New Mexico capital Santa Fe, but the direction of travel is unclear, perhaps because of the joint that he contemplates smoking. The driver might either be 90 miles to the east of Santa Fe – from Route 66 this would be near Santa Rosa, New Mexico – or, having arrived in Albuquerque, he could be thinking about an alternative route back on Route 85 through the mountains of Colorado. Disorientation after a long journey is signalled by the distance only being hearsay (he begins with the colloquial phrase 'Well, they say . . . ') and by the tight internal rhyme of the opening couplet. The song stresses physical and spiritual hunger, overlain with a desire to escape that harks back to his anonymous arrival in the country. His urge to stop for ham and eggs is perhaps a yearning for Canada or a comforting symbol of home that could sustain him on his journey. This need for sustenance is poignant because Young fainted soon after arriving in Albuquerque and had to seek hospital treatment for symptoms of onset epilepsy – a condition that plagued him during his time in Los Angeles.

A few days later Young felt well enough to leave Albuquerque. He lightened the load on Mort II, leaving behind two travellers, Jeanine Hollingshead and Tannis Neiman, who had been irritating him on the journey, and Mikey Gallagher, who was weary of the trip (Hollingshead and Neiman eventually found their own way to Los Angeles; Gallagher returned to Canada). That left Young, The Mynah Birds' bassist Bruce Palmer and their Yorkville friend Judy Mack to finish the drive. The remaining 780 miles to Los Angeles through the Mojave Desert passed largely without incident, although the black hearse was always likely to attract the interest of law enforcement officers. This heightened Young's feeling of paranoia, particularly as Palmer was casual about carrying his stash of marijuana.

After the trials of the road the travellers drifted into Los Angeles on a foggy April Fools' Day, tired from driving flat-out from Albuquerque. Judy Mack took a bus back to Canada almost as soon as they arrived, while Young and Palmer slept in Mort II before crashing at a friend's place near Laurel Canyon Boulevard.[1] The Los Angeles that Young recognized at first was one that he had seen on Canadian television. He was initially 'giddy' and overwhelmed by the experience, looking for familiar landmarks such as the sign for 77 Sunset Strip, the name of the private detective series that he had watched as a teenager.[2] The duo's search for Stills proved frustrating during their first week and they resorted to selling rides in Mort II – that is, until Stills and Richie Furay spotted the hearse on Sunset Boulevard just moments before the two Canadians were about to abandon the city and head up the coast to San Francisco. The meeting has been heavily mythologized, not least because the success of the five-piece Buffalo Springfield was remarkably and unexpectedly rapid.[3] Stills, Furay, Young and Palmer were joined on drums by another Canadian, Dewey Martin, who had arrived in Los Angeles via Las Vegas and Nashville two years earlier.

When Young reflects on his arrival in Los Angeles in his songs it tends to be in very individualistic terms, rather than as part of a group experience. Perhaps the clearest expression of this is the opening track on *Harvest*, 'Out on the Weekend', recorded in Nashville in April 1971 with The Stray Gators, five years after Young's arrival in LA. The opening metronomic drum beat and gentle country guitar push forward the rhythm, but the harmonica melody in the key of A that joins after fifteen seconds is at once aching and expectant. The simple opening line, 'Think I'll pack it in and buy a pick-up', begins 40 seconds into the song. Hovering between purposeful action and the fantasy of escape, it is a thoughtful line despite its apparent simplicity. The ten monosyllables hang on the two plosive 'p's and three 'k's ('think',

Neil Young was in residence on Skyline Trail in Topanga Canyon from 1968–70.

'pack' and 'pick'), but the hard rhythm is softened by the half-rhyming 'I'll' and 'buy'. The casual opening phrase is reinforced by the blue-collar vehicle, while the regular chord shift between A and B minor in the verses makes the journey to Los Angeles both carefree and melancholic. This is also signalled by the transition in the lyrics. The breezy drive down the Pacific Coast (emphasized by the vocal stress on the two syllables of L–A) is replaced in the chorus with the image of the drifting singer. The optimism of buying a pick-up truck and finding a new home is tempered by the singer's loneliness, despite the affectionate woman who lingers on his mind. It is a song of arrival and expectation, but the singer is in danger of collapsing into wordlessness or a state of exhaustion. In fact, the affectionate woman might well be a personification of Los Angeles itself: she seems to be the answer to the singer's desires but is also a site of melancholy and loneliness.

This sense of ambivalence was reflected in the status of Los Angeles in the mid-1960s as a place of countercultural ferment and an unstable city on the verge of eruption. The opposition was epitomized in geographical terms by the junction of Sunset Boulevard and Laurel Canyon Boulevard, where the excitement of the recently established LA club scene met the steep, winding climb from the Canyon Country Store up to Mulholland Drive in the Hollywood Hills, connecting city and wilderness, before dropping down to the San Fernando Valley. Young lived close by the Country Store in the early days of Buffalo Springfield and then moved to a cabin on Utica Drive part-way up the climb (near Stills and Furay), before retreating further from what he called the 'big phoney scene'of Hollywood.[4] In summer 1968 he relocated 20 miles or so away to a redwood house with a view on Skyline Trail in bohemian Topanga Canyon, where he lived with his first wife, Susan Acevedo.

As the site of the folk rock scene between 1965 and 1969 Laurel Canyon was much mythologized: The Mamas and the Papas sang of the move from a drab New York City to the pastoral haven of the Canyon on their 1967 single 'Twelve Thirty'; Jim Morrison pictured Canyon Country Store as the place 'where the creatures meet' on The Doors' 1968 track 'Love Street'; and Joni Mitchell was to immortalize the area with her album *Ladies of the Canyon*, released in March 1970, by which time the musical community had already started to disperse. But in the mid-1960s the creative interaction between the songwriting activities of Laurel Canyon and the club circuit of the 1.7-mile-long Sunset Strip was unprecedented for the Pacific Coast. If Toronto's Yorkville offered a creative meeting point for the folk revivalists and the emerging folk rock scene in the mid-1960s, then the intersection between Sunset Strip and Laurel Canyon was an even more exciting crossroads of culture and commerce.

The historian Kevin Starr points out that Los Angeles was defined by its car-friendly boulevards after the Second World

War, in contrast to the distinct neighbourhoods of San Francisco. Despite attempts to make LA a recreational city from the 1920s onwards, post-war urban development was rapid, 'moving south, west, east, and north horizontally across the plain, ceasing only at mountains and sea' as planners tried to keep pace with population growth.[5] But the tranquillity of Laurel Canyon in the mid-1960s was an exception to this urban sprawl, following a spurt in housing development over the previous 30 years. The musical and artistic community that settled there after 1964 (when LA's first folk-rock band The Byrds moved in) could find in 'the canyon's rugged granite walls and cool, quiet night air sweetened with jasmine and acacia blossoms' a haven from the commerce and racy nightlife of Sunset Strip.[6] Life on the Strip was, in contrast, an ongoing conflict between the burgeoning youth culture and a vigilant police force. Drinking licences for bars and clubs, traffic problems and rowdy behaviour kept police officers busy, especially in the summer and autumn of 1966, when they tried to enforce a curfew after 10 p.m. for anyone under the age of eighteen.[7] The closing of Pandora's Box coffee house at the junction of Sunset Boulevard and Crescent Heights Boulevard led to ugly scenes and a number of arrests in November, as captured in the low-budget film *Riot on Sunset Strip*, released the following spring.[8]

Stills depicted this clash between law enforcement and the youth scene in Buffalo Springfield's second single 'For What it's Worth', in which 'the children' and 'the heat' are caught in an epic battle between two very different ways of life. The song's sympathy rests with the outspoken youth and warns them to listen for danger as they might do a coastal invasion or the threat of a Cold War bomb. Although the song had significant radio airplay when it was released in January 1967 (and it made number 7 on the national charts), 'it isn't exactly clear' what the children stand for and there is no mention of the Vietnam War as a unifying cause behind which they could rally – or any reference to other incidents

Publicity photograph of the original line-up of Buffalo Springfield, 1968.

of urban unrest, such as the Watts riots the previous August.
Creeping paranoia suggests that the song is a warning against
the dangers of being coerced by abstract authority, rather than
a straightforward protest or a strident call for organized action.
Its relevance was heightened by the fact that around this time
the long-haired Young was arrested (on the pretext that he had
outstanding parking fines) and treated roughly after offending an
officer and Bruce Palmer was deported temporarily to Canada in
1967 (following previous arrests for drug possession).

If Laurel Canyon was a hub of musical creativity in the mid-
1960s, then Sunset Strip provided the opportunity for Buffalo
Springfield to emerge as one of the most exciting North American
bands of 1966. What is remarkable is that their first gig on 11 April
at The Troubadour club on Santa Monica Boulevard – a club

'where everyone met, where everyone got to hear everyone else's act', according to Linda Ronstadt – happened only twenty days after Young and Palmer had left Toronto.[9] The band took its name from the side of a parked steamroller, but the name also captured the dispersed geography of its five members, comprising three Canadians, a Midwesterner and an itinerant Southerner. The five-piece was tight harmonically but symbolically loose, projected by their distinct images: Stills's Stetson hat and jacket contrasted with Furay's Beatles-like image, Palmer's mysterious Beat demeanour and the buckskin leather of Young's 'Hollywood Indian' persona. With two accomplished singers in Furay and Stills, Young's initial role was as a charismatic guitarist who played tightly with Palmer and developed a call-and-response pattern with Stills's blues rhythms.[10] With songs ready to go Stills and Young quickly established an energetic set list for Buffalo Springfield's seven-week stint that summer as the house band at Whisky a Go Go on Sunset Strip, where they often played alongside The Doors.

Despite the initial excitement of forming a new band and their distinctive harmonies (in which Chris Hillman of The Byrds showed particular interest), Young's experience with Buffalo Springfield was not as fulfilling as he had expected. Management wrangles troubled the group from the outset and the respect between Young and Stills soon turned into rivalry. The pair duelled with each other onstage as guitarists, particularly during the extended guitar solo of 'Bluebird', and also offstage as they sought control of the band. Young often praises Stills, calling him a 'genius' with an 'amazing groove . . . like a clock with a feel, never rushing or dragging', but this respect did not prevent the two from sparring.[11] Young later thanked his first manager, Ahmet Ertegün, for not retaining them both on Atlantic Records because their infighting had become explosive by 1968. Certainly, his position in the group changed more than the others. On the eponymous debut album, released in December 1966 (reissued in March 1967,

this time with 'For What it's Worth' as the opening track), Furay
provided vocals for Young's songs, but Young soon began to sing
his own material, believing that his hesitant voice was more suited
to the complex lyrics than Furay's mellifluous tones.

Young's urge to be assertive was complicated by the epileptic
seizures that he started experiencing in autumn 1966, including
one mid-set seizure on 2 September 1966 at a gig at Melodyland,
Anaheim.[12] The clinical status of his epilepsy was indisputable.
But Stills believed that he play-acted at times to attract attention,
even though the fast, staccato rhythm of 'Mr Soul' seemed to
trigger further seizures and occasional blackouts at the end of
gigs. 'Mr Soul' can be read as a song about the physical and
mental effects of industry pressure as his head and face disappear
in a whirl of uncontrolled movement. George McKay has noted
that the effects of epilepsy are reflected in a number of Young's
lyrics, such as the stumbling singer in 'Expecting to Fly' and the
fragile figure who tries to stay up while running down the road
in 'Out on the Weekend'.[13] Fragility is also evident in 'Out of My
Mind', the penultimate track on Buffalo Springfield's debut album.
This delicate song attributes emotional breakdown and suicidal
thoughts to the 'screams' of fans that plague the singer 'from
outside the limousines'; the queasy internal rhyme ('screams',
'limousines') reveals an urgent need to flee reality. The struggling
figure in the song experiences an out-of-body experience, perhaps
stimulated by marijuana or by prescription drugs that were
increasingly part of Young's life. Whatever the source of these
lyrics, the frenetic pace of life from autumn 1966 through to
spring 1968 (when Buffalo Springfield split) affected Young's
health and coloured his general response to Los Angeles.

When he speaks about Los Angeles it tends to be in very
broad, almost abstract terms. 'LA was just real big' and 'couldn't
get anything together in LA', he told Jimmy McDonough in the
early 1990s, almost as if he was an embodiment of the figure

in 'Out on the Weekend' who struggles to speak.[14] This lack of articulacy might be unfavourably compared to the expressive poetry of Dylan in the mid-1960s, but it might alternatively be linked to the geography of Los Angeles itself: 'a sprawling, fragmented metropolis' that is difficult to map with any certainty.[15] This phrase, drawn from Cécile Whiting's book *Pop LA* (2006), follows architect Ken Lynch's claim in *The Image of the City* (1960) that Los Angeles is 'hard to read' and where even the rational downtown grid system is 'an undifferentiated matrix, within which elements cannot always be located with confidence'.[16] Lynch's interviews with Los Angelinos in the late 1950s revealed a general sense of dissatisfaction with the downtown; it was seen to be less harmonious, 'greyer' and 'more abstract' than other areas, perhaps due to its generic storefronts and smog. This was a far cry from the hippie haven of Laurel Canyon and is expressed in 'Don't Let it Bring you Down' as a swallowing-up of nature: the 'blue moon' sinks 'from the weight of the load' as lorries roll by.

The image of a dystopian city is best expressed in 'LA', the fourth track on *Time Fades Away*, written in 1968 and recorded live at the Myriad, Oklahoma City, in March 1973. Young's rough vocals reveal an alarming meditation on downtown Los Angeles. The chorus focuses on urban smog and feelings of being uptight (perhaps a reminder that Young's epilepsy intensified during his four years there), while the line 'don't you wish you could be here too?' is an ironic commentary on Southern California as a tourist destination. The irony comes through strongly as the city is paradoxically both stifling and on the verge of eruption.

I will return to 'LA', but it is worth pausing on the title track of Young's second solo album *Everybody Knows This Is Nowhere*, his first project with Crazy Horse (formerly The Rockets), with whom he had only played for a few weeks before starting to record the album. The title track is one of the album's tighter compositions, but fresh air blows through it. The two-and-a-half-minute song does not name Los Angeles explicitly; instead, it contrasts a 'cool and breezy' image of home to living in a city of frenzied activity. This urge to escape links to the album cover, which depicts a relaxed musician in the mountains wearing a plaid shirt and leaning against a tree with his half-husky Winnipeg as his companion. This cover image is perhaps a wish fulfilment because Young's nervy urban sensibility was often on show at the time; in fact, up close the clear visual image is virtually a series of tight pointillist dots that create a more disorienting impression. Instability is also the chief factor for wanting to leave the scene on 'LA', but uneasy feelings also pervade the melancholic opening track of *After the Gold Rush*, 'Tell Me Why', as the singer contrasts the tedium of making arrangements to the imaginative dream imagery of 'heart-ships' and 'broken harbors'. The upbeat tempo and easy country guitar of 'Everybody Knows This Is Nowhere' belie a discomfort with a city that is both everywhere ('a city without boundaries', according to urban theorist Mike Davis) and nowhere (echoing the title of Alison Lurie's LA novel *The Nowhere City* from 1965).[17]

There is certainly a dystopian slant to Young's Los Angeles songs, but also more positive features that complicate his response to the city. This echoes the distinction that Cécile Whiting makes between Ken Lynch's concept of an indecipherable city and Reyner Banham's 1971 field study of the metropolitan area. Although Banham shared Lynch's concern that car culture had 'shrivelled the heart out of downtown', he pictures a city that benefits from diversity rather than suffering from lack of definition.[18] Banham outlines four ecologies – beach and coastline, mountains, central valley, and the freeway – and suggests that Los Angeles can only be understood in its variety rather than from a fixed urban point.[19] Just as Pop artist Ed Ruscha captured the detail of cultural life in his documentary art book *Every Building on Sunset Strip* (1966), so the notion of LA as an assemblage of parts characterizes another aspect of Young's response to the city.

We see this reflected in the image on the front cover of Young's first solo album. Producer and arranger Jack Nitzsche (who had worked closely with Phil Spector and helped to develop the Wall of Sound) encouraged Young to leave the band because he did not think it was allowing him to flourish as a singer-songwriter. After a couple of temporary splits with Buffalo Springfield in 1967, Young started working on a solo project the following summer, with Nitzsche and Wyoming-born David Briggs as his co-producers. The album, *Neil Young*, was released on Reprise Records in November 1968, four months after Buffalo Springfield's final release *Last Time Around*, the cover of which shows Young looking the opposite way to the other four band members. In contrast, the cover portrait for *Neil Young* is of a solitary singer positioned right of centre at the meeting point of metropolis, desert and sky. The portrait was painted by local artist Roland Diehl in Topanga Canyon, where Young had recently moved to relax in the mountains and to gain some distance from the city.

The cover image is composed around three horizontal bands, each of which blends into Young's head and shoulders. The bottom band is of an inverted modern city in green (corresponding to Lynch's description of the 'piling-up of blank office structures' in downtown Los Angeles) set against the backdrop of a brown and blue night sky, which might equally be urban smog.[20] Two geometric buildings blend subtly with the singer's wavy, shoulder-length hair, but the other buildings are held back by the strong crescent of Young's neck, which reflects the lighter yellows of the desert and sky. The middle band is the most stable. Here, desert and mountain frame the singer's face and are mirrored in the contours of his cheek bones and eye-lines, making him paradoxically both old and young. The upper band of the picture shifts from the bright yellows of the setting sun in the top left through a diagonal of oranges that blend into the purple and marine blue of the top right-hand corner. The psychedelic

Cover of Young's debut solo album, *Neil Young* (1968), based on a Topanga Canyon painting by Roland Diehl.

sky picks up on the darker swirls at the bottom, but the vibrant colours highlight the singer's hair and connect the coastline and canyon, revealing an elemental force that the city cannot swallow. Rather than representing the sprawl of the city, this portrait is one of creative metamorphosis. It erases the hard boundaries between the singer and his southwestern environment, but also prefigures the contrasting ecologies that Banham identified in his reconceptualization of Los Angeles three years later.

This idea of the city as a place of connection comes through strongly in 'LA'. The first verse refers to the coast, not the city, and the reference to a 'friend' perhaps refers to a group of Canadian travellers that Young and Palmer met in Santa Monica on their arrival in spring 1966 – although it might equally be an ironic use of 'friend', conjuring instead the kind of duplicitous and hollow Mr Jones figure who features in Dylan's 'Ballad of a Thin Man'. The image of the ground cracking at the end of the first verse might refer to the southern section of the San Andreas Fault, which passes 35 miles north of Los Angeles. Although a version of the track was written in 1968, the San Fernando earthquake of February 1971 and the world's deadliest earthquake off the coast of Peru in May 1970 might have given Young pause for thought ahead of its release on *Time Fades Away*: the effects of the former were quite localized, but the Peruvian earthquake was a major natural disaster, causing more than 70,000 deaths. This reference is relevant given the convoluted imagery of the second verse, where 'the bubbles in the sea' give rise to an 'ocean full of trees'. The eruption might equally be a symbol of urban instability, reprising the clash of cultures on Sunset Strip in 'For What it's Worth'; the song suggests that the whole region might erupt only minutes after the 'friend' has arrived in the city. It is certainly not a positive track and the city's instability seems to be unstoppable. The natural and urban disaster is linked closely to the invective against the 'friend', who turns out to be a similar tormenting figure to the one that is evoked in the first verse of 'Nowadays Clancy Can't Even Sing'. Nonetheless, as an expression of the region's intersecting ecologies, 'LA' is more complex than it first appears.

The coastal area of Southern California is sometimes linked closely to Los Angeles in Young's music, and at other times offers a stark contrast. 'Cowgirl in the Sand', for instance, the closing, ten-minute electric guitar track of *Everybody Knows This Is Nowhere*, written during a bout of illness while resident in Laurel Canyon, is both specific (this was the first coastal area that Young had lived in and the Western theme filters through the image of the cowgirl) and mythological (Young mentioned in London in 1971 that when he wrote the song he was thinking of Spanish beaches). 'Cowgirl in the Sand' moves through four long guitar sections, which in 1969 a *Rolling Stone* reviewer called 'alternately soaring, piercing and driving', and the three verses seem like dream fragments where the singer cannot quite wake up to reality or fix the image of the woman he desires in his mind.[21] This sleepy mood is conveyed through disorientating colour moods, swirling from the yellow sand and dust to the reds of 'ruby' and 'rust' in the second verse (hinting at the orange-brown imagery of the opening track 'Cinnamon Girl') to the intriguing 'purple words on a grey background' in the third verse. The purple is perhaps a reference to Young's colour blindness, which made it hard for him to differentiate between red and blue, but it also links to the indecipherability that he frequently associates with Los Angeles. This, then, is a more internal and abstract form of instability to that of 'LA', but similarly one where Southern California drifts in and out of focus as real and fantasy landscapes slide into each other.

Los Angeles is also both present and absent on tracks on Young's 1974 album *On the Beach*. The album's eight tracks were recorded in San Francisco and Hollywood, by which time urban Los Angeles was more of a memory for Young than any kind of home. Even though he was resident on Sea Level Drive, north of Malibu, while writing and recording this album, he tried to keep away from the city. *On the Beach* can be treated as a critique of celebrity (Young finds himself uncomfortable and alone at the microphone during a radio interview on the title track) or a meditation on the fading hippie dream (on 'Revolution Blues' he personifies Charles Manson, whom he knew briefly and whose brutal murder of the pregnant actress Sharon Tate and six others shattered the peace of Laurel Canyon in August 1969).[22] The album hovers between serious commentary on contemporary

A 1974 advertisement for Neil Young's album *On the Beach*.

politics and culture and the brooding, introspective mood. This is
exemplified by the title track, on which he looks inwards to escape
from a world that threatens to turn against him or to spin out of
control – the song ends with the singer steeling himself to leave
town, perhaps for the last time.

The mixture of apocalypse and mystery is signalled by,
arguably, Young's most enigmatic album cover, created by his
long-term collaborator Gary Burden. Shot at Santa Monica
Beach, the singer looks away from the city towards the Pacific
with a lonesome pair of boots positioned a few metres from
him. In the foreground a yellow Cadillac is buried in the sand
with only its tailfin on show, near a newspaper front page with
a headline about Richard Nixon. Released three weeks before
Nixon's resignation as the nation's 37th president, the album
captures the pessimism of the Watergate years, but also reflects
Nixon's prominence in Los Angeles: he was born in Yorba Linda,
southeast of the city, was a California senator in the early 1950s
and opened the Anaheim theme park Disneyland as Eisenhower's
vice-president in 1955. Young was to treat Nixon with more
sympathy on his mid-1970s track 'Campaigner'. Recorded initially
with the more apocalyptic title 'Campaigner (After the Fall)',
this reflective song credits the disgraced president with having
at least a modicum of soul. However, *On the Beach* pictures
Nixon as a symbol of sharp decline from the high ideals of the
1960s: he appears as a shady and deceitful figure on the final
track, 'Ambulance Blues'. This jaundiced mood is captured in
the cover's colours of muted yellow and blue, but this is wrapped
together with a resilience that endures despite the turns of
history and circumstance. This resilience is reflected in a 1974
advert for the album when the mood of the cover shifts from
melancholy to engagement as Young smiles toward the camera
against the backdrop of Santa Monica Beach. A resilient undertow
is also evident on the collection of songs: we are invited to 'walk

on' (rather than falling over) on the opening track and are warned about those who say 'good times are coming' on 'Vampire Blues'. As one of Young's most bluesy records (three tracks have 'blues' in the title), the album pushes the listener to think about the seductions and pitfalls of a world that rarely makes sense.

The fact that Young intended to release an album titled *Oceanside–Countryside* in the mid-1970s and returned to the topography of the west, as depicted in roadie James Mazzeo's sketch for the *Zuma* album cover and in his nostalgic train song 'Southern Pacific', shows that he thought seriously about geography and did not reduce the region to its principal city. In fact, the cultural life of Los Angeles is resuscitated somewhat via Young's interest in cinema, even though his film references usually contrast with slick Hollywood productions (which he described as being 'buried by the neon') and his own projects deliberately have a rough, unfinished quality.[23] His film-making aspirations led to his first film, *Journey through the Past* (1972), a *cinema-vérité* documentary heavily influenced by French New Wave director Jean-Luc Godard, whose montage techniques are evident in his 1968 Rolling Stones' film *Sympathy for the Devil*. In addition, Young's third solo album, *After the Gold Rush*, was linked to an unrealized film project based on a script by fellow Topanga Canyon resident Dean Stockwell (later a collaborator on *Human Highway*), which would have blended potential apocalypse with New Age spirituality.[24] The southwest is present and absent in both cases. *Journey through the Past* cuts from rough tour footage to virtually empty images of the Mojave Desert, and Young claimed that *After the Gold Rush* was influenced by the spirit of Topanga Canyon: its title track focuses on the dream of escaping from a 'burned-out basement' in a silver spaceship that has the power to transport humans to a 'new home in the sun'.[25]

The most obvious film reference is on the penultimate track of *On the Beach*, 'Motion Pictures (For Carrie)', dedicated to his then partner (and mother of Zeke), the film actress Carrie Snodgress. Young portrays watching TV films as 'a home away from home', a form of 'livin' in-between' that helps to connect him to Carrie. The song is full of longing and melancholy, but 'motion pictures' have the therapeutic potential to pull the singer out of himself via a form of externalized fantasy. This is in contrast to the *Harvest* track 'A Man Needs a Maid', where cinema is linked to internal fantasies, as Young reflects on falling in love with Snodgress. The film reference to her Academy Award-winning role of a frustrated New Yorker in *Diary of a Mad Housewife* (1970) is barely recuperative, though, as the disconnected singer contemplates the benefits of a functional and service-based relationship. The song ends with a moment of tenderness when he asks 'When will I see you again?', but it is not clear whether this is a fantasy or a real love temporarily out of reach. This gloom is especially relevant, as it turns out, because Young was taking painkillers for a severe back complaint while writing the song, and he admits that cracks in his relationship with Snodgress were there even before the recording of *Harvest* was complete.[26]

It is clear that Los Angeles was a major turning point for Young, even though he found the experience both frustrating and physically debilitating. His retreat 360 miles up the coast to La Honda in 1970 might have saved his health, but it also prevented him from developing a sharper view of the city's rapid urban development and worsening civic problems. Nevertheless, in a group of songs written between 1966 and 1974 we can see the city as an embodiment of two important elements discussed in the introduction: first, the figure of the rootless musician who drifts through intersecting scenes; and, second, the notion of 'détournement' in which Los Angeles is constantly turning from one thing to another. The dystopian city that we see in 'LA' did not carry through strongly to other songs in this group, except for the hateful reference to the Laurel Canyon community on

'Revolution Blues', as seen through the dark hippie eyes of
Charles Manson.[27]

When Young came to reflect back on the LA scene in his
1979 track 'Thrasher' it was with enough clarity to see that the
hippie dream was over in the city.[28] The poetic phrase 'lost in
crystal canyons' (possibly targeted at David Crosby, whose drug
addiction was rampant by the late 1970s) reveals a hedonistic and
self-medicating Laurel Canyon community that has abandoned
its quest for musical vibrancy. This turn away from the LA
community's early ideals prompts the singer to hit the road again
and escape to 'where the pavement turns to sand'. However, these
negative feelings should be placed alongside a more affirmative
response to the broader geography and interconnecting ecologies
of the southwest. The opening song of the 1978 album *Comes
a Time*, 'Goin' Back', for instance, pictures creative harmony
between mountains, rocks and city buildings, while the mysterious
'caves' and 'caverns' of 'Light a Candle', the most contemplative
track of his 2009 release *Fork in the Road*, suggest that the
southwest has primitive resources that cannot be ignored.

3 THE DEEP SOUTH

Neil Young's two memoirs, *Waging Heavy Peace* (2012) and *Special Deluxe* (2014), are a testament to his two lifelong loves: cars and music. In one of the most joyful sequences of *Waging Heavy Peace* we see him driving on a Californian highway and enjoying the debut album *Hell on Heels* by the three-piece Nashville group Pistol Annies. The other major trio in the book, Crosby, Stills & Nash, are not treated so sympathetically, despite their long-standing relationship with Young which started in August 1969, a few months after his collaboration with Crazy Horse began. The tight harmonies of CSN and the barroom guitars of Crazy Horse are two musical poles between which Young has often shuttled during his career. This has led him to compose delicate songs like 'Helpless' for CSNY's album *Déjà Vu* (1970) and muscular guitar tracks, beginning in 1969 with 'Down by the River' through to his most recent album of new material with Crazy Horse, *Psychedelic Pill* (2012). The longest track on that album, the 27-minute jam 'Driftin' Back', does not revisit any of his major collaborations (Buffalo Springfield, Crazy Horse, CSN, Farm Aid), but instead reflects upon the process of writing *Waging Heavy Peace* and Young's dislike of digital sound. This passion for improving musical quality contrasts starkly with the inferior streaming channel Rhapsody on which he listens to Pistol Annies during his car journey.

It is perhaps surprising, then, that he greets the Nashville trio with so much enthusiasm, especially when their sound is based on their stage presence and vocals rather than their musicianship. Perhaps the band speaks to Young's desire to write new music (he was suffering from songwriter's block at the time) or his passing wish to work within a tight genre. Perhaps it is a reflection on growing old: he exclaims that 'I love hearing this energy. I recognize it from my own youth, and it gives me faith in life and makes me feel.'[1] Or perhaps it is an unconscious attempt to revive the image of the South after it had taken a beating in two of his songs of the early 1970s, 'Southern Man' and 'Alabama'.

This chapter is slightly different to the previous two and the next one because Young has never lived in the South. With The Squires he performed an idiosyncratic version of the mid-nineteenth-century minstrel song 'Oh! Susanna', which recounts a banjo player's troubled journey from Alabama to Louisiana in search of his true love, but as a young man he was only dimly aware of the region until Buffalo Springfield ventured outside of California in 1967. They played Texas, Arizona, Nevada and Virginia that year, and then supported The Beach Boys on a nationwide tour the following April, including concerts in the Carolinas, Florida, Georgia, Oklahoma, Arkansas, Louisiana and Alabama. In 1969 Young identified Tulsa as his representative American place (perhaps because the Oklahoma city is located on the edge of the Great Plains), but his route into Southern culture was via Nashville, Tennessee.[2] In February 1971 he recorded songs for *Harvest* at the Quadrafonic Sound Studios with the newly assembled country group The Stray Gators, the same month that he played two new songs at Vanderbilt University for the *Johnny Cash Show*, 'The Needle and the Damage Done' and 'Journey through the Past'. He then returned periodically to record and play in Nashville over the next 40 years, including the *Homegrown* sessions at the Quadrafonic in late 1974. Over his career he has tended to polarize the South: at times he depicts it as an inward-looking and intolerant region, and at others he respects its

vibrant cultural heritage, embodied in the musical legacy of
Hank Williams Sr and Elvis Presley.

Early in his solo career Young relied firmly on his instincts
when it came to assessing the region. This is illustrated in his
vague description of his 1970 track 'Southern Man' in the liner
notes of *Decade*. He writes that 'this song could have been written
on a civil rights march after stopping off to watch *Gone with the
Wind* at a local theater', before admitting that 'I wasn't there so
I don't know for sure.' This vagueness could be seen to make
him unqualified to comment on the South and at a significant
remove from the realities of activism and conflict in the region.
Alternatively, it could be seen to give him an imaginative licence
that more extensive knowledge might have constrained. The
choice to focus on the South seems to have been his own, despite
the encouragement of David Crosby and Graham Nash to write
more politicized songs. But he would certainly have benefited
had he read studies such as Lewis Killian's *White Southerners*
(1970), which presents a varied region and tries to avoid crude
caricatures.[3] He might have been aware of the psychiatrist Robert
Coles's fieldwork on desegregation in Southern schools (published
in the *Atlantic Monthly* in 1967) or accounts of rural and small-
town poverty that appeared in the mass media in 1969, but there
is little evidence that Young read extensively about the South.
The fact that his music was not heavily influenced by the blues
tradition suggests that his engagement was generally with the
white South rather than a deep immersion in African American
culture – or, at least, that the blues is just one musical tradition
within his hybrid soundscape.

His lack of deep social and cultural engagement with the
region meant that he shared the widespread West Coast prejudice
towards the white South at the turn of the 1970s, as illustrated in
the depiction of intolerant rednecks in Dennis Hopper and Peter
Fonda's *Easy Rider* (1969). But Young's response cannot be easily

stereotyped. For example, he audaciously chose to play 'Southern Man' in 1973 at Louisiana State University (a tour on which he also played in Tuscaloosa and Mobile, Alabama), but then veered away from this scathing attack on racial intolerance after witnessing a violent clash between a black policeman and a white fan during an Oakland Coliseum concert of 31 March 1973. He dropped the song from his set list after his next gig in Sacramento, only reviving it on a Crazy Horse tour of Japan and Europe in 1976, and then as part of his back catalogue in the 2000s.[4] This might be seen as a sign of Young's growing sensitivity to the South, which led him to play Southern venues more frequently and to collaborate with outlaw country artists Willie Nelson and Waylon Jennings. However, it is important not to see his treatment of the South as an aberration. That he has continued to write about conflict and war suggests that these Southern songs are one aspect of a broader trend and not a unique case. This links 'Southern Man' and 'Alabama' to his response to the violent reaction of the National Guard towards the student protests at Kent State University against President Nixon's expansion of the Vietnam conflict into Cambodia on the 1970 single 'Ohio', through to his outspoken stance against u.s. intervention in Iraq on his 2006 album *Living with War* – an album which caused a backlash among conservative concertgoers when Young toured it with csn on the 2006 Freedom of Speech tour.

Before looking closely at Young's Southern tracks, it is worth pausing on 'Ohio', the 'greatest protest song ever' according to a 40-year anniversary piece in *The Guardian* and an example of his ability to identify injustice in other regions.[5] Young wrote 'Ohio' quickly in May 1970 after Crosby had showed him an advance copy of *Life* magazine with the headline 'Tragedy at Kent', focusing on the death of four students and the injury to nine others on 4 May at the hands of the National Guard, some of whom were not directly involved in the protest against the invasion of Cambodia. This was Young's first song to combine politics and feeling in equal measure. He regarded it as his best CSNY track, perhaps because the hippie and dawning activist within him joined forces for the first time.[6] This allowed him to fuse an elegy for lost youth with a militarized song, signalled by the heavy opening rhythm in dropped D and the memorable first line, in which President Nixon is subordinated to his hollow army. 'Ohio' is both powerful and tender, shifting from observation to active engagement and involving the listener in the events of the song.

The shifting pronouns are the most interesting lyrical feature of the song, moving from 'we' to 'I' to 'us' to 'you' over the course of two verses. The first two lines switch from the students who warily observe the advance of the 'tin soldiers' to the detached singer who hears the drums of war. The second verse is more ambiguous. The phrase 'Gotta get down to it' could be from the perspective of the advancing soldiers, or perhaps the Kent State students as they try to organize their protest against the military intervention. The second line about the brutality of the soldiers is clearly spoken by the students, but the third – 'Should have been done long ago' – could equally be an expression of impatient authority or the students considering more militant forms of protest. The verse then prompts listeners to think about how they would react on discovering a murdered body, triggered by student Howard Ruffner's *Life* cover photograph of the wounded student John Cleary being tended by three others (Young incorrectly remembers that this image was one of the dead four, Allison Krause).[7]

The two verses, taken together, offer an example of Young's montage technique as he works through the moral, political and human consequences of the bloody encounter by inhabiting different points of view. Recorded at Record Plant Studios in Los Angeles on 15 May, the poignancy of 'Ohio' is heightened by Stephen Stills's elegiac anti-Vietnam War track 'Find the Cost of Freedom' on the flip side of the single. Stills had written this haunting song with its a cappella ending for the closing sequence of *Easy Rider*. It did not make the final cut of the film, but helped to push the single to number 14 on the national chart in June 1970 – and was later recycled as the coda of another track written by Stills, 'Daylight Again', in 1982, which revisits the Civil War from the historical perspective of a Southerner.

'Southern Man' is musically more complex than 'Ohio' and stands out on *After the Gold Rush* in its focus on racial conflict and in harking back to the soaring guitars that punctuate the verses of 'Down by the River' and 'Cowgirl in the Sand'. The song begins abruptly, almost as if Crazy Horse has been playing the riff for some time and someone has just remembered to turn on the microphone. Young's vocals are intense throughout and allow no emotional relief. He combines the role of a bard-like figure who can see history and geography clearly from a distance and a Baptist preacher who reminds Southerners to remember the teachings of the Bible. An attack on religious hypocrisy as much as racism, the song looks forward to social change in the region, which was even more necessary in the wake of the two assassinations of 1968: the civil rights leader Martin Luther King Jr in Memphis in April and Bobby Kennedy in Los Angeles that June (Kennedy had recently conducted poverty tours of the South). Rather than writing a topical song mourning the death of two leaders who promised reform (as Crosby does on the elegiac 'Long Time Coming'), 'Southern Man' rails against a culture of racial violence, ongoing persecution by the Ku Klux Klan, and an intolerant mentality embodied in the white Southern backlash to desegregation. The KKK can be glimpsed in the song carrying 'burning crosses' and the Klan is obliquely referenced by the dark-hooded horsemen that appear riding on the beach in *Journey through the Past*, a film which also includes an impassioned CSNY performance of 'Southern Man' accompanied by the aerial shot

L–R: Stills, Nash, Crosby and Young (with Dallas Taylor and Greg Reeves) rehearsing in 1970, photographed by Henry Diltz.

of a plantation.[8] But compared to the careful scene-setting and precise location of 'Ohio', actual incidents of racial hatred are only implicit in the song.

The vibrant colours that characterize the first two solo albums are here replaced by stark black-and-white imagery. The first observational lyric contrasts white mansions and cotton fields with 'little shacks' and black fieldworkers who regularly receive the bullwhip. Just like Stills in 'Daylight Again', Young sees the past and present simultaneously. But rather than prefiguring Stills's elegy for dead Confederate soldiers, no one in 'Southern Man' emerges with any dignity. The shifting point of view is more stable than it is in 'Ohio', but 'Southern Man' equally moves between time frames and perspectives. In a scene reminiscent of the rape sequence in D. W. Griffith's classic silent film *Birth of a Nation* (1915), the first half of the final verse is seen through

the eyes of a white plantation owner who pictures a southern
belle with golden hair (the only colour image) supposedly being
threatened by or even in love with a black worker. Either way, it
triggers the plantation owner's hateful plan to 'cut him down'.
The 'I' in this racially stereotyped scene is clearly an impersonated
voice because the verse soon returns to the distressing sound of
screams and 'bullwhips cracking'. Here, though, the screaming
is a discordant blend of black and white voices and the sound of
whipping is sexually charged. The shouted question 'how long?'
powers through the song and is levelled as much at stereotypes of
black violence as the ongoing oppression of African Americans.
What, then, seems at first to be a song written by a northern
migrant who has little knowledge of the South emerges with a
subtlety that is often overlooked.

Another way of approaching 'Southern Man' is as a more
universal expression of conflict that links up to the rocking anti-
Vietnam War song 'Sea of Madness' (played at the Woodstock
Festival by CSNY) and the aching piano ballad 'Soldier' from
the soundtrack album *Journey through the Past*. But rather than
focusing on conflict abroad, 'Southern Man' brings the issue close
to home by exposing ongoing violence in the South, in a similar
vein to Nash and Young's single 'War Song' of 1972, which links
combat overseas and on the streets. These tracks set the tone
for later songs, particularly 'Shock and Awe' (2006), which rails
against the hypocritical public statements of leaders during the
Iraq War, and 'War of Man' (1992), which fuses past and present,
this time stimulated by the earlier military intervention in the
Persian Gulf. Sometimes Young shouts angrily at the president,
the army or a regional mentality, but 'War of Man' reflects
philosophically that 'no one wins'. He reinforced this perspective
in a rambling interview with Jimmy McDonough in which he
compares 'extremist' factions in Canada and the Deep South,
before noting that the relevance of 'Southern Man' had waned by

the mid-1990s, prompting him to switch his target towards 'White Man' in general.[9]

A more immediate comparison to 'Southern Man' is 'Alabama', one of the most absorbing tracks on *Harvest* and which Young performed live with The Stray Gators on *Journey through the Past*. The track begins with Young cranking out his electric guitar before the drums kick in, almost as if an old car is firing up. The song feels like a musical account of a road trip, but rather than any precise geographical coordinates we are presented with an imaginative drive, with a few hints of cultural and political history on the way. The chorus suggests that the Cotton State is breaking up from the 'weight of the Union'. This can be read to mean that either the federal government should put pressure on Alabama to mend its old ways, particularly on racial issues, or that the state had been left in poverty and 'ruin' too long, leaving it economically twenty years or more behind northern states.

The arresting image of a Cadillac with one 'wheel in the ditch' and the other 'on the track' suggests that all is not lost, while images of the cultural past offer a positive contrast to the startling images of 'broken glass' and 'white ropes'. This does not amount to the diatribe of 'Southern Man'. Instead Young's tender intonation of the song title, the offer of a handshake and his admission that he is an outsider who comes in friendship reveal a generosity that his songs sometimes lack, leading Johnny Rogan to describe him as a 'reasoning liberal' promoting the message that isolationism is not the way forward.[10]

Whatever subtlety we read into 'Southern Man' and 'Alabama', the two songs unsurprisingly led to recrimination among white Southern listeners. The most obvious backlash was on 'Sweet Home Alabama', the opening track of Lynyrd Skynyrd's album *Second Helping* (1974). As one of the band's best-known songs, 'Sweet Home Alabama' is often seen as straightforward praise for the South, a sentiment that propelled

it to number 8 on the national charts. 'Mister Young' is introduced
in the second verse as an outsider who does not understand
Southern culture. But rather than a sustained attack on the
Canadian, the song is equally critical of intolerance, booing
Governor George Wallace, who had given Alabama a bad name
by refusing to uphold the racial integration of public services
and schools. This is in contrast to positive images: blue skies,
the open road and home-grown music – the latter in the shape
of the Muscle Shoals Sound Studio northwest of Birmingham,
where Lynyrd Skynyrd recorded their debut album in 1973. The
reference to the Muscle Shoals' house band The Swampers
and the honkytonk piano which rounds out the song means
that the reference to Young is left far behind. In contrast to the
critical attitude of the West Coast music fraternity to the South,
journalist Mark Kemp notes that the opening lyric 'big wheels
keep on turning' is drawn from Creedence Clearwater Revival's
track 'Proud Mary' (1969), which credits Southerners with an
authenticity that seemed to be in short supply in California.[11]

Young accepted the criticism that he got the South wrong –
he had actually stopped performing 'Alabama' live in 1973 before
'Sweet Home Alabama' was written, and he never performed it
again except for a medley of the two songs at a Miami concert a
month after the plane crash that killed Lynyrd Skynyrd's singer
Ronnie Van Zant and two other band members. Nevertheless, the
contrast between the northern Young and the Florida-born Van
Zant has come to define 1970s rock music. Van Zant recognized
that Young was mainly just criticizing corrupt authority in the
South, but reputedly said in 1976 that he felt he was 'shooting all
of the dogs because some had some flu'.[12] However, the fact that
Young wrote 'Powderfinger' and 'Sedan Delivery' with Lynyrd
Skynyrd's 1976 album *Gimme Back My Bullets* in mind, and Van
Zant wore a *Tonight's the Night* T-shirt for a July 1977 Oakland
concert (as well as under his cowboy shirt on the cover of his

Ronnie Van Zant of Lynyrd Skynyrd wearing a *Tonight's the Night* T-shirt in concert, Oakland Coliseum, Oakland, California, 2 July 1975.

final album *Street Survivors*), suggests that this caricature of a war between West Coast rock and Southern rock has been grossly exaggerated.[13]

This incident has nevertheless become part of the mythology of the South. The most obvious illustration of this is Alabama band Drive-By Truckers' 2001 concept album *Southern Rock Opera*, which revisits the clash between 'Ronnie and Neil' as one of the defining moments of the 1970s. The Muscle Shoals sound is seen as distinctively Southern, but its 'brand of commercial R&B' had national influence, attracting a host of musicians in the late 1960s and 1970s: Percy Sledge, Wilson Pickett, Aretha Franklin, The Rolling Stones and The Osmonds all recorded hit singles there, and Bob Dylan chose the studio to record his *Saved* album in 1980.[14] Set against this cultural vibrancy Young's criticism of the South is seen as unwelcome and out of touch. Drive-By Truckers credit him with speaking 'some truth' about the region, but the charge against him is that his focus on the 'bad shit that went down' (as described in the song) overlooks the positive features of Southern culture. However, Young is not wholly dismissed as an intruder. In fact, not only do the Drive-By Truckers acknowledge that Lynyrd Skynyrd were actually fans of Young, but the band also mourns the demise of guitar-based rock as embodied in the mythical clash between 'Neil' and 'Ronnie'. Further evidence that musical battle lines of the 1970s were drawn too starkly is revealed by Gregg Allman's admission that Young's Buffalo Springfield songs inspired him; by The Allman Brothers Band's decision to play an extended version of 'Southern Man' on their 2012 tour; and in Gov't Mule performing an eight-track Neil Young set at a 2014 Christmas Jam in Asheville, North Carolina.[15]

Young's suspicion that the South represented American intolerance at its very worst occasionally resurfaced, such as the image of 'the man' breaking in half his 'silver fiddle' during a visit to Dixie on 'See the Sky about to Rain' (1974), a track that he demoed in the *Harvest* session two years earlier.[16] But the post-revolutionary mood that fuelled his albums between 1973 and 1975 is rarely as culturally specific as it is in the tracks written at the turn of the decade. This reflects Jerome Rodnitzky's claim in 1971 that 'blatant message music' was disappearing in 'an age of polarization, fragmentation, and general discord'.[17] More importantly Young's growing fascination with country music was a major factor in his mellowing towards the South. The interest in folk culture was there from his early days in Canada, but his exploration of country emerged strongly in 1977–8 on *American Stars 'n Bars* and *Comes a Time*, and then resurfaced in the mid-1980s in a more sustained form on *Old Ways* and through to later albums. It also highlights a central tension in Young's work between his recognition that the South has a special sense of place, and what Martyn Bone describes as a 'postsouthern' interrogation of the cultural myths of the region.[18]

Harvest capitalized on the aura of Nashville and was important in bringing Young mainstream success, even though the musicianship of The Stray Gators was unfavourably compared in the press to the rhythm section of Crazy Horse on *Everybody Knows This Is Nowhere*.[19] This is unfair on The Stray Gators, particularly Ben Keith, whose steel guitar and musicology were reliable resources for Young over the next four decades. *Harvest* drifts in and out of country, hanging on the coat-tails of Gordon Lightfoot's 1967 Nashville recording *The Way I Feel* and recent country albums by Bob Dylan and The Byrds. Dylan's *Nashville Skyline*, including the Johnny Cash duet 'Girl from the North Country', was especially influential and pointed to 'the future of country music' as a de-regionalized and hybrid genre.[20] The same was true for The Byrds' Gene Clark, who fused country and rock in his collaboration with bluegrass banjo player Doug Dillard, and for a post-Clark Byrds on the country album *Sweetheart of the Rodeo*, inspired by their new Southern singer Gram Parsons.[21]

Young was also keen to work within this mode. He recruited East Coaster James Taylor and Arizona-born Linda Ronstadt (who both played alongside him on the same episode of *The Johnny Cash Show*) as backing singers for 'Heart of Gold' and 'Old Man', and he chose to record *Harvest* at a range of studios in Nashville, London, Los Angeles and Northern California. Following the plodding cover of Don Gibson's 1958 lament 'Oh Lonesome Me' on *After the Gold Rush*, only the title track of *Harvest* and 'Are You Ready for the Country?' could be called true country songs, enhanced by vocals from Crosby and Nash. The persistent question in 'Are You Ready for the Country?' is a gentle call to his fans to recognize that roots music had travelled across the region in multiple directions, from the neo-country sound of Bakersfield, California (often called the 'Nashville of the West'), during the 1950s and early 1960s, to the fusion of country, folk and rock up and down the Pacific Coast in the late 1960s.[22] 'Are You Ready for the Country?' is also an example of Young having fun – a carefree mood that carries through to the outlaw country singer Waylon Jennings's honkytonk cover four years later, which made number 7 on the country charts.

Jennings re-emerged as a collaborator on *Old Ways* a decade later, one of the albums Young released while trying to extract himself from the Geffen label. Set against other genre albums he made in the 1980s, *Old Ways* does not look strange. The International Harvesters developed an old-time country sound with which he had first flirted in the late 1970s on *Comes a Time*. But the album was, for some critics, associated with Young's perceived shift to the political Right. This was fuelled by his public statement in support of President Reagan in 1984, although a few years later he claimed that he was not 'a Reagan supporter in a total blanket sense' and was neither liberal nor conservative.[23] More tangibly, the album coincided with the launch of Farm Aid, which was a major expression of Young's affiliation with agrarian America. But whatever the precise motivation, *Old Ways* could be seen to be a more natural successor to *Harvest* than his 1992 album *Harvest Moon*, which self-consciously reworked his signature album twenty years on.

Some song titles on *Old Ways* are oddly clichéd, as if Young was revisiting the genre knowing that Western and Southern traditions had blurred and that the South could no longer claim to own its music in a nativist sense, as evident in the titles of 'Where is the Highway Tonight?', 'Californian Sunset' and 'Are there Any More Real Cowboys?' The third song links up to his concern for the American farmer as a contemporary working cowboy and family man struggling against the capitalist system, a theme echoed in an *Old Ways* session track 'Depression Blues' and the title track of his latest album *The Monsanto Years* (2015). A *Rolling Stone* review suggested that Young might be sending up the genre by singing with an 'audible smirk', but the album spans too many emotions to reduce to a single message.[24] Its hybrid quality is marked by the inclusion of Jennings and Nelson, two of Nashville's outlaws more closely associated with Texas than Tennessee; that year the pair formed the supergroup The Highwaymen, with Johnny Cash and Kris Kristofferson, to shake off 'the false, squeaky-clean image of country entertainers'.[25]

As an album *Old Ways* lacks the craft of Young's more acclaimed releases, probably because he had ditched an earlier version when Dave Geffen had complained about it being untypical. Nevertheless, in glimpses it shows his talent for working as a genre musician. This is best illustrated by 'Get Back to the Country', a song which blends his early success with Buffalo Springfield and a joyful celebration of roots music. The International Harvesters mix of traditions, including Ben Keith's pedal steel and the Louisianan Rufus Thibodeaux's Cajun-influenced fiddle, lend 'Get Back to the Country' a live feel that makes it both a travelling song and an answer to the question

posed thirteen years earlier in the title of 'Are You Ready for
the Country?'. The album and the 1984–5 North American tour
(encompassing concerts in Georgia, Tennessee, Louisiana and
Texas) gave Young the opportunity to sing about his children and
time passing, with the mawkish 'My Boy' sitting alongside the
exuberant 'Amber Jean', a celebration of his newly born daughter
and the opening track of the musical document of the tour,
released as *A Treasure* in 2011.[26]

Young came to realize that Southern music – particularly
the so-called 'Nashville Sound' – was not a singular tradition
and that its journey to and from the West Coast had taken many
routes that led him both towards Southern roots and away from
them towards working-man western songs like 'Southern Pacific'
and 'Union Man' at the turn of the 1980s. His musical responses
to the South became more subtle and varied as he matured, in
contrast to the impassioned tracks released at the beginning
of the decade. The fact that the home of country music, the
Grand Ole Opry, regularly presented a 'cross section of nearly
every American musical form' (music critic Paul Hemphill lists
bluegrass, honkytonk, gunfighter ballads, Cajun music, rock 'n'
roll, mountain spirituals, cowboy songs and pop) meant that the
Nashville Sound was more a loose label than a musical blueprint.[27]
When Young came to play at the Ryman Auditorium, the site of
the Grand Ole Opry from 1943 to 1974, with a talented country
band in mid-August 2005 (as captured in Jonathan Demme's
film *Neil Young: Heart of Gold*), it was with the awareness that he
was just one musician working within a complex and changing
tradition. But he also believed that his northern and western
roots did not prevent him from making a valuable contribution
to country music.

While Young probes and coaxes us to look beyond the
mythologies of the South, the counter-trend of seeing Southern
music as exceptional is filtered through the figures of the

Young playing his Martin D-28 guitar, 'Hank', at the Ryman Auditorium, Nashville, April 2005; still from *Neil Young: Heart of Gold* (dir. Jonathan Demme, 2005).

Alabaman Hank Williams Sr and the Mississippian Elvis Presley – two iconic figures who drift in and out of Young's songs from the late 1970s and feature on two tracks he played at the 2005 Ryman Auditorium concerts. The presence of this pair is linked closely to Young's growing recognition that Southern influences are complex threads and that Southern music cannot easily be demarcated by place: Williams was 29 when he died in 1953 on the journey back to Tennessee from a New Year's concert in Ohio, suffering from fatigue and the long-term effects of pills and alcohol, while in August 1977 a bloated and disintegrating Elvis died in Memphis in the middle of the night following a recent cabaret stint in Las Vegas.

The passing of Elvis ('the King' on 'Hey Hey, My My') is testament to the exuberance and the dangers of a rock 'n' roll lifestyle. It is not clear in 'Hey Hey, My My' whether Elvis is an example of an artist who burned out or faded away (probably the latter), but when Young returned to his childhood idol on the 1983 rockabilly album *Everybody's Rockin'* it was to a theatrical version of Elvis, complete with quiff and a pink suit.[28] Young retained his affection for the man who diverted him from his childhood plan of becoming a chicken farmer. He launched his return as a rocker in September 1989 with a blistering performance of 'Rockin' in the Free World' on *Saturday Night Live* wearing an Elvis T-shirt under his leather jacket (with a faint echo of Presley's leather-clad 1968 comeback), and in the early 1980s he named his Tennessee bluetick coonhound after Elvis, as immortalized on his banjo song 'Old King' (1992).[29] When he came to revisit Presley's legacy in 2005 on 'He was the King' for the *Prairie Wind* album he did so both affectionately and playfully. On this track Elvis's many faces – rock star, gospel singer, film actor, cabaret performer, frontman for a country band and Cadillac enthusiast – mean that it is impossible to pigeonhole the King of Memphis.

The same is true for Hank Williams, whose country blues emerge as one of Young's two musical directions on the opening track of *Harvest Moon*, 'From Hank to Hendrix', offering an acoustic counterpoint to the histrionic guitar blues of Jimi Hendrix.[30] The most tangible connection between the pair is Young's purchase of Williams's 1941 Martin D-28 acoustic guitar in the mid-1970s. The tender relationship that developed between Young and the instrument is evident on another *Prairie Wind* track, 'This Old Guitar', and in a close-up image of its sound hole on the album's lyric sheet. During the Ryman concerts he expressed his delight that Williams's guitar was returning to its home at the heart of Nashville and he claimed that he had always tried to do the 'right thing by it', even loaning it to Dylan for a time.[31] Taking good care of the guitar makes it responsive to Young's moods, but he also realizes that he will forever be a musical apprentice to it.

In a 1992 interview he reflected on the importance of 'Hank' as an instrument and an icon ('it's always great to realize the history you are holding in your hands'), stressing that he did not want it to become a museum piece but to remain part of a living culture.[32] Rather than a strong feeling of ownership or a sense that only Southern musicians have a right to play Williams's guitar, he recognizes that it has its own journey and is only passing through his hands for a time. Ultimately, Young sees the guitar both as an authentic object to be cherished and an old companion that has travelled 'up and down the country roads' with him – and on Hank Williams's lost highway before him.

4 NORTHERN CALIFORNIA

Two Neil Young and Crazy Horse recordings from the 1990s best characterize Young's attitude towards the coastal region around San Francisco. The most recent of the songs is 'Big Time', the electrifying seven-minute opening track of the album *Broken Arrow* (1996), named after Young's La Honda ranch, tucked away near the Pacific Coast west of San José and south of Santa Cruz. 'Big Time' returns to Young's American journey. But rather than retelling his 1966 road trip from Toronto to Los Angeles he takes a different route, picking up the story he started on 'Thrasher'. This trip is not a realistic drive up the West Coast in his 'old black car', though, but in 'Big Time' it is a mythical journey travelling 'state by state' in search of San Francisco and what in *Special Deluxe* he mythologizes as the 'North Country'.¹ The lyrics of 'Big Time' are tongue-in-cheek: this is the land of 'suntan lotion' where he can take a 'magic potion' that allows him to glimpse a mermaid in San Francisco Bay. Even so, it is sung with the earnest belief that the dream he held as a young man can still be realized. The song is one of extremes, as if this stretch of coast embodies the defining American contradictions that Walt Whitman had identified over a century before Young arrived in California.

The second of the two tracks is 'Mansion on the Hill', written six years earlier and one of the most memorable tunes on *Ragged Glory*. It opens with a direct reference to 'Old Man', a song he composed on moving to La Honda and released as a single in April

1972. The figure in the title is not his father Scott Young (who was then 54) but Louis Avila, a caretaker who lived on the ranch before Young acquired it. Meeting the elderly caretaker prompts him to think about his age, his home, his future, and his luck in becoming a young 'rich hippie'.[2] When he revisits the same visual image in the first verse of 'Mansion on the Hill' twenty years later (when Young was in his mid-40s), he sees the old man of his earlier song 'walking in my place', as if he now wears the caretaker's shoes.

Despite the moment of recognition, this is a distinct person, not a mirror image of Young. The wild-eyed figure appears to be a refugee from the late 1960s – reminiscent more of Jerry Garcia of the Grateful Dead than the dark hippie Charles Manson – who wants one more shot at recreating the era of love and peace. The figure is a catalyst for a cosmic journey, transporting the singer from the 'road of tears' to a 'highway to the sun', where time and space open up into wide vistas of coast and mountains. 'Mansion on the Hill' echoes the title of Bruce Springsteen's nostalgic track on his largely bleak 1982 album *Nebraska*, as well as one of Hank Williams Sr's most lonesome songs, here turned into an affirmative vision of community. It could also be seen as a wry retelling of a founding American myth, its phrasing echoing the second Governor of Massachusetts Bay Colony John Winthrop's vision of a 'city on the hill'. And rather than mirroring the luxurious resorts emerging on the Pacific Coast, such as the expensive Post Ranch Inn (which opened in 1992), 75 miles south of Santa Cruz, the mansion morphs into a communal house reminiscent of the Grateful Dead's legendary Haight-Ashbury residence between 1966 and 1968. 'Mansion on the Hill' does not settle on a distinct location such as Big Sur or Golden Gate Park, but remains within a generalized natural setting where 'psychedelic music' drifts from the house.

As with many Young songs, there is little narrative progression in the two verses of 'Big Time' and 'Mansion on the Hill'. A reflection on a place and an era that is not yet over nevertheless pulses through the two tracks. This contrasts starkly with his jaundiced take on the period in his 1986 track 'Hippie Dream'. Here we see Young in ultra-cynical mood, taking a shot at 'Wooden Ships' from csn's debut album of 1969. David Crosby co-wrote the track with Jefferson Airplane's vocalist Paul Kantner, in which they imagine a nuclear apocalypse whereby North America (or possibly Southeast Asia) has become contaminated with radiation in the aftermath of war. Leaving behind the cries of the 'silver people on the shoreline', wearing radiation suits as they try to stave off death, the pair of sailor refugees escape in a wooden boat after surviving for weeks on a meagre diet of purple berries. One of csn's most popular concert songs, 'Wooden Ships', was also recorded by Jefferson Airplane for the *Volunteers* album of 1969; on this version the dialogue between the two escaping companions – one from each side of the war – is attenuated by Paul Kantner's and Grace Slick's contrasting vocals and fades into a celebration of the magical power of music. This is in contrast to csn's coda, where Crosby whispers that a 'fair wind' will blow the boat away from the mainland to an uncontaminated island to the south.

Young played guitar on 'Wooden Ships' for csny gigs in the early 1970s, but the disillusioned mood that pervades *On the Beach* and *Tonight's the Night* intensified in the 1980s. There is just a glimmer that the dream can be resuscitated in the bridge line of his 1986 track 'Hippie Dream', but Young thought that the pure waters of the mid-1960s counterculture had been contaminated with egoism, greed and drugs.[3] He wrote 'Hippie Dream' at a time when Crosby was at a low with his drug habit: he was freebasing frequently during studio sessions, was often losing consciousness, and was in court in 1982 on cocaine and weapons charges – the paranoia in his hippie anthem 'Almost Cut My Hair' having intensified after the murder of John Lennon.[4] Crosby skipped rehab in 1983 and was imprisoned for

five months in 1985 after causing a car crash while freebasing at
the wheel. Young refers obliquely to this episode and Crosby's
love of boats in 'Hippie Dream', bemoaning that the 'tie-
dye sails' of the 1960s are now lost in a world of imprisoning
addiction. Rather than seeing 'Wooden Ships' as a creative
collaboration between Southern and Northern California
(embodied in the co-writing credits of Crosby and Kantner),
Young plays the high-handed moralist, claiming that 'the dusty
trail' of enlightenment has been lost and the hippie dream
'capsized by excess'. Returning to his early anti-drug songs
'Flying on the Ground (is Wrong)' and 'The Needle and the
Damage Done', the track ends at possibly his bleakest moment:
the image of an abject 'flower child' in an anaesthetized abattoir.

The exuberance of 'Big Time' and 'Mansion on the Hill'
is more typical of Young's response to California, but 'Hippie
Dream' is a useful, if disturbing, counterpoint because it contrasts
the sourness he experienced in Los Angeles with his feeling
of freedom further up the Pacific Coast Highway. Northern
California did not completely escape his cynicism. For example,
his role as the San Francisco motorbike salesman Westy in the
low-budget movie '68, released to an underwhelming reception
in 1988, shows that the mid-1980s was a jaundiced time for Young. In
contrast to the idealism of the two young Hungarian immigrants,
Peter and Sandy Szabo, who experience the sexual liberation of
late-1960s San Francisco in all its complexity, Young's character
is a middle-aged, gum-chewing miscreant who orders Peter to
take down a campaign picture of Bobby Kennedy that the activist
student had posted in the workplace. In a particularly crude
moment Westy dismisses the pacifist Democratic Party candidate
Eugene McCarthy (whom the folk trio Peter, Paul and Mary
had championed in their 1968 'Eugene McCarthy for President'
campaign song), mistaking his surname for that of the Cold War
Republican red-baiter Joe McCarthy.

Neil Young as the San Francisco motorbike salesman Westy in a publicity still for *'68* (dir. Steven Kovacs, 1988).

Whereas a number of Young's and CSNY's songs formed the soundtrack to the 1970 radical student protest film *The Strawberry Statement* (the album sleeve describes Young as 'the necessary man'), the return to the countercultural moment of the late 1960s from the more conservative perspective of the late 1980s saw him playing a character who is part of the problem rather than the solution. The role of Westy is another example of

Young challenging his audience. It also distances him from what many of his generation saw as a halcyon moment that had been destroyed by the rise of authoritarianism and the emergence of the New Right, rather than the self-destruct impulse that he identified in the mid-1980s. It was not until the aftermath of 9/11 and the invasion of Iraq in 2003 that Young's political voice returned forcefully. But his invective against reckless drug use and his cynical character in '68 shows that he cannot be easily pigeonholed as a nostalgic hippie.

Nonetheless, Northern California was a positive move for Young. The decision to buy a 140-acre ranch in the rural community of La Honda was primarily to escape the pressures he felt in Los Angeles. On moving there in September 1970 he found that his health recovered rapidly away from the 'day-to-day running around' he sings about on 'Everybody Knows This Is Nowhere'. Not only was this a private retreat far enough away from urban life, but it allowed Young to build a recording studio, to indulge his passion for cars and to live out his childhood dream of being a farmer by rearing livestock. One view of Broken Arrow Ranch was as a sealed fiefdom with a hint of magic, 'a Ponderosa for sensitive people', according to photographer Joel Bernstein.[5] Young's plan to build a recording facility based on Nashville's Quadrafonic Studios meant that he could regulate his working hours and cultivate a support team more easily than he could in other locations. His choice to settle in a rural area that was new to him but also reminiscent of his Canadian past might seem to be the antithesis of the travelling musician. However, the ranch was a hub through which he could tap into the creative spirit of the Bay Area community without losing himself in it.

Ironically, perhaps, Young was missing on the first occasion when he might have participated in such a communal event. The Monterey Pop Festival took place in June 1967 at the height of the so-called Summer of Love, which had begun early in the

year in Golden Gate Park. The festival, which is remembered
for the explosive antics of Jimi Hendrix and The Who, attracted
an audience of 50,000, many of whom enjoyed free LSD tablets,
renamed Monterey Purple for the occasion (LSD became illegal in
California in autumn 1966). Young had temporarily left Buffalo
Springfield a few weeks earlier and Stills invited Crosby to sing
with the band (he struggled to keep up with the lyrics), together
with The Daily Flash guitarist Doug Hastings. Buffalo Springfield
preceded The Who and the Grateful Dead on the festival's final
day and played a six-track set including 'Nowadays Clancy Can't
Even Sing', with Richie Furay on vocals, and a tame version of
Stills's 'Bluebird'. However, only the opening track 'For What
it's Worth' was filmed and their songs did not feature in D. A.
Pennebaker's landmark film *Monterey Pop*, perhaps because the
cobbled-together band was not as cohesive as they were with
Young in the line-up.[6]

Joel Selvin describes the Monterey Festival as 'an axis on
which the world of rock music turned', whereas Barney Hoskyns
views it more sceptically, seeing it as a clash between the divergent
cultures of Los Angeles and San Francisco, and arguing that
it was 'effectively a rock 'n' roll trade show masquerading as
a love-in'.[7] Psychedelic rock was certainly not free from the
commercial pressures that sullied the LA scene for Young. But
the Grateful Dead were keen to embrace a different spirit of
community by developing an 'anticorporate, community-based
image' and staging free concerts in Golden Gate Park, including
the Summer Solstice 'Do-In' concert of 21 June 1967, supported
by The Diggers and the Hells Angels and using amplifiers and
speakers liberated from the Monterey concert.[8] The Dead's rented
home at 710 Ashbury Street also housed the Haight-Ashbury
Legal Organization, which offered free legal advice to members
of the hippie community to go alongside the free news, free food
and free transportation facilitated by The Diggers. The Dead

hoped that 'small moral communities [would] continue to grow'
and that urban post-industrial groups would promote the pre-
industrial values of rural settlements, because 'these families
represent the true nature of all future people who are presently
subjugated by the paid-off and unaware community.'[9] This is
one of the most powerful expressions of communal ideals of the
time, leading critics to characterize experiments in group living
in Haight-Ashbury, Sausalito and Ocean Beach as embodiments
of 'the energy, alternative values, and ecology necessary to
sustain an independent protest deprived of official standing'.[10]

Young initially felt on the outside of the San Francisco scene,
but the Dead's interest in 'electricity' and their anti-corporate
ethos appealed to him, even though the theme of community
took time to emerge in his music.[11] Instead, his early years were
marked by a mixture of strident individualism and uncertainty.
He could blend into different groups fairly easily, but he always
seemed a loner, as the second track on his debut solo album
announced (even though 'The Loner' has often been interpreted
as a song about Stills). Young soon strained against the musical
direction of The Squires and in some CSNY concerts he seems to
be a brooding fourth presence with no fixed place on stage.

Given that the Grateful Dead were always bigger as a band
than as a group of individuals puts distance between them and
Young. In fact, the direct links between Young and the Grateful
Dead are fairly limited: he name-checks the band on his *Psychedelic
Pill* track 'Twisted Road', and they played briefly together in 1991
for a rendition of Dylan's 'Forever Young' at a Golden Gate Park
tribute concert for the legendary San Francisco concert organizer
Bill Graham (during a period when Garcia was trying to recover
from a heroin and cocaine habit almost as severe as Crosby's
addiction). But their broader cultural connections have been
underexplored, perhaps because Young admitted in *Shakey* that
the group did not initially make much of a musical impression

on him: 'it took years' for him to appreciate the Dead's subtlety
or 'even just to realize what it was'.[12] In *Special Deluxe* he reflected
that 'he was late or had missed the moment or something, just
a little out of place' when he played at The Warfield theatre in
San Francisco in early 2001, 'where the Grateful Dead played a lot
back in the day'.[13] This sense of being out of time or coming to
the scene slightly late resonates through Young's life, as we will
see with his arrival in La Honda. But we will also see how the
band hovers in the background of Young's one complete concept
album: his 2003 release *Greendale*. Not only did the Grateful Dead
epitomize the blending of rock, folk and progressive country that
characterized the late-1960s West Coast sound, but they embodied
two ideas that recur through Young's career: they deliberately
wrote drifting music and they refused co-option by turning
against a corporate mentality.[14]

Young did not move up the West Coast to buy into a
particular philosophy. He never wholly sided with either the
left-wing faction of the folk revival or the more conservative
culture often associated with country music. Nor did he indulge
in the New Ageism that appealed to many hippies, despite the
cosmic imagery that occasionally surfaced in his songs, most
obviously in the 'silver spaceships' of 'After the Gold Rush', and
his participation in a concert at the Esalen Institute, a mystical
therapeutic retreat on the dramatic Big Sur coastline not far
from the open bohemian commune Gorda Mountain. Esalen
was an early outing for CSNY, just a month after they debuted
as a four-piece at the Woodstock Music and Art Fair. The Big
Sur Folk Festival had been running since 1964 at Esalen and the
September 1969 event (documented in the film *Celebration at
Big Sur*), was not heavily politicized, despite a fur-coated Stills
being lured into a fight with a stoned hippie when he was
accused of having sold out. Young played a slightly off-key
'Sea of Madness' and an exuberant 'Down by the River' with

The Pacific coast at Julia Pfeiffer Burns State Park, overlooked by the Esalen Institute, Big Sur, California.

the trio, enhanced by Greg Reeves on bass and Dallas Taylor on drums. But he did not feature centrally in an event where the romance between Nash and Joni Mitchell was on obvious display and Crosby enjoyed the therapeutic benefits of a group sauna. The Esalen Institute was distinctly anti-corporate, but this only fed through in terms of the tuned-out audience and its proximity to the unspoiled beauty of the coast. There were no political slogans or causes at the concert, aside from a group performance of 'Let's Get Together' and Joan Baez's powerful rendition of 'Song for David', a song about her activist husband David Harris who had been imprisoned that July for refusing the draft.

The Esalen concert was diametrically opposite in spirit to another free festival at which CSNY played that year, mainly because the Big Sur crowd was limited in number by the landscaped grounds of the Institute, bounded by cliffs and the sea. On 6 December 1969 CSNY played a four-song set as a prelude to the Rolling Stones at the Altamont Speedway Free Festival, located in the northeast corner of the San Francisco Bay Area and touted to be the West Coast's answer to Woodstock. The CSNY set included 'Long Time Gone', Crosby's homage to the recently assassinated Bobby Kennedy, and another rendition of Young's 'Down by the River' that touches on what turned out to be an appropriate theme of violence and passion.

CSNY left the makeshift stadium quickly after their set when they heard that the Grateful Dead had pulled out because a member of Jefferson Airplane had been hurt by a Hells Angel. The choice of the renegade Californian motorcycle club as security was relatively uncontroversial given that they coexisted peacefully with hippie groups and had helped the Dead stage free concerts in Golden Gate Park. Violence came to a head a few songs into The Rolling Stones' set, though, when the large crowd pressed close to the badly designed stage. Following numerous scuffles, eighteen-year-old Meredith Hunter was knifed by a Hells Angel after twice trying to mount the stage and threatening to pull out a revolver. This murder of an African American youth, together with three other accidental deaths, meant that Altamont is rarely remembered for its music (other than the Stones' performance, featured in the 1970 documentary *Gimme Shelter*). CSNY were only part-players in an event that is widely viewed, along with the Manson murders, as one that killed the idealism of the 1960s. But the fact that CSNY was the only group that linked the pastoral retreat of Esalen to the ugly violence of Altamont makes the band central to the story of the unravelling of the hippie dream.

Young has never commented directly on Altamont (unlike the Grateful Dead, who wrote 'New Speedway Boogie' the following year in response to the disastrous festival), and his songwriting at the beginning of the 1970s rarely revealed the bleak soul-searching that characterized his ditch trilogy – *Time Fades Away, On the Beach* and *Tonight's the Night* – in mid-decade. However, the violence of 'Ohio' and 'Southern Man' was very likely inflected by the abrasive events that had begun to erupt across the country. The creative legacy of the times was also long-lasting. While overtly politicized songs faded from his writing after 1974, he cultivated an anti-corporate stance that was to punctuate the remainder of his career. Until much later he was rarely as musically radical as the Grateful Dead (although they too tried to remain politically unaffiliated) and he did not adopt the anarchist collective spirit of The Diggers or the socialism of other community action groups.

This is an important aspect of another idea discussed earlier. Young's ragged aesthetic not only emerged in fits and starts, but mirrored the diverse strands of West Coast counterculture, its influences 'cobbled together, disjointed, and intertwined with mainstream values'.[15] As such, he moved between songs that celebrated rural life and experiments with technology which avoided the slick, radio-friendly arrangements that came to dominate Californian rock in the mid-1970s. We can find other examples of this desire to blur experimental and mainstream music, such as Crosby's 1970 song 'Tamalpais High (At About 3)', a track which celebrates the natural calm of the Bay Area's most iconic peak, Mount Tamalpais, and drifts wordlessly around a group of musical themes, perhaps influenced by the contributions of Jerry Garcia's tonal guitar and fellow Grateful Dead member Phil Lesh's versatile bass. Nevertheless, Young explored this current in more sustained and subterranean ways than his peers.

The Dead were involved in a now legendary cultural happening that connected the San Francisco scene directly to La

Honda. In 1965 and the early part of 1966, Ken Kesey, author of
One Flew over the Cuckoo's Nest and then resident in a two-bedroom
log cabin in La Honda, conducted a series of all-night acid tests.
These events involved his group of friends, the Merry Pranksters,
recently returned from a coast-to-coast trip in their psychedelic
bus, as well as the Beat figures Allen Ginsberg and Neal Cassady.
The Pranksters could be seen as a self-chosen community that
placed its faith in spontaneity and creativity, stimulated by heavy
doses of psychedelic drugs. They felt a natural kinship with their
chosen house band, the Grateful Dead, because the technique
of 'playing songs longer and weirder, and louder' (as Garcia
described it) was an appropriate soundtrack for the acid tests.[16]
The Pranksters also deployed the Dead's lighting designer, Del
Close, in order to create a multimedia backdrop for the communal
trips, linking to what Kesey called the 'neon renaissance' of
psychedelic festivals such as the three-day Trips Festival in January
1966 at the Longshoreman's Hall in San Francisco.[17] Tom Wolfe,
who documented the La Honda happenings in *The Electric Kool-
Aid Acid Test* (1968), noted that the Dead 'did not play in *sets*', but
'might play one number for five minutes or thirty minutes. Who
kept time? Who *could* keep time, with history cut up into slices',
stimulated by the intake of LSD.[18]

Wolfe was particularly interested in the La Honda location
and his account of the area might well have appealed to Young:
'Strategic privacy. Not a neighbour for a mile. La Honda lived
it Western style. Not to be seen from scenic old Route 84.'[19] If
Young had read on then he would perhaps have been deterred by
the mention of the Berkeley crowd that periodically descended
on the area, and Wolfe's description of the place as an 'intellectual
tourist attraction' once word of the Merry Pranksters' activities
was known.[20] And nor was Young drawn to hallucinogens, based
on his doctor's serious warning when he was first treated for
epilepsy in Los Angeles. Nevertheless, Wolfe's description of an

attractive and private redwood area that was both part of the 'raggedy-manic Era' and yet at one remove from it would have been appealing.[21] There is no evidence that Young knew Kesey. The Oregon-born author still owned the log cabin when Young bought his ranch 12 miles away in 1970, but by that time Kesey had lost interest in the Merry Pranksters, refusing to join them on their trip to the Woodstock Festival, and he had started to tire of communal living.[22] Kesey became more private after spending five months in jail in Redwood City for marijuana possession. Soon afterwards he retreated up the coast to the Willamette Valley in Central Oregon, although he did not sell his La Honda home until 1997. The fact that La Honda possessed a countercultural vibe appealed to Young, but by the time he arrived the freshness and optimism of those heady experimental days was on the wane.

Neither the erosion of a generational cause nor the size of his estate prevented Young from appreciating the simplicity of rural life. His new lifestyle triggered memories of his Canadian upbringing, as reflected in 'Journey through the Past', one of the early tracks he wrote in La Honda. A simple but ecologically conscious song on his debut solo album, 'Here We are in the Years', also values the slow pace of the country and the joys of seeing 'the sky without the smog', while 'Country Home' (a track he wrote in the mid-1970s but did not release until it appeared on *Ragged Glory*) credits the city as having 'lots of style', but it proves tiring and cannot sustain him like the country can. Repeatedly through the 1970s – from *Harvest* through to *Rust Never Sleeps* – Young returned to the beauty and calm of the natural world. One of his most memorable but also most casual songs, 'Homegrown', the closing track on his 1977 album *American Stars 'n Bars*, could be read as a celebration of growing your own marijuana, but it is more broadly a pioneering commitment to working with the land, resonating with the early days when La Honda was a tiny settlement. The lyrics seem to have been written at a single sitting and show Young at his most colloquial as we see the sun shining on crops that 'start jumping up' out of the earth. He planned 'Homegrown' as the title track of an unreleased country rock album recorded in late 1974 and early 1975 in Nashville; the plan was to release *Homegrown* with an old-time cover depicting a young peasant boy playing a harmonica corn-cob to his faithful dog. Other rural tracks written for the album, including 'Deep Forbidden Lake' and 'The Old Homestead', appeared as part of other projects later in the decade, which, together with another unreleased concept album, *Oceanside–Countryside*, reveal his close affinity with life in La Honda.

We might read this trajectory as Young settling into a comfortable groove in the mid-1970s after losing faith with the counterculture and following the burst of creativity of his early solo albums. But this was far from the case: while Young was never as adventurous and carefree as the 'Intrepid Traveller' – the name the Merry Pranksters gave to the laughing countercultural guru Ken Babbs – he continued to explore musical journeys despite firmly setting down roots in La Honda.[23] We have already seen how Young drifted around country music in the 1970s and challenged the expectations of his record label, fellow musicians and fans alike, as he did when he released the proto-punk *Tonight's the Night* rather than the country rock album *Homegrown*. This musical drifting seems to correlate with the shifting status of home for Young: he is never entirely at home despite his long-term residence at Broken Arrow Ranch. Even if his early years in Canada tug at a depth of emotion that he rarely displays towards his adopted American home, the San Francisco Bay Area is not a single place but, like the southwest, is full of convergences and intersections. For example, his choice of the Bay Area as a setting for two of his more accomplished songs of the 1990s, 'Mansion on the Hill' and 'Big Time', was a prelude to his imaginative return to the geography of Northern California on the 2003 concept album *Greendale*.

Advertisement from 2003 for the Neil Young and Crazy Horse album *Greendale*.

At first glance *Greendale* looks like an anomaly. Described in publicity as a 'musical novel', instead of pursuing a theme or loose concept the album relates the story of three generations of the Green family in the fictional Northern Californian coastal town of Greendale.[24] The generations have different value systems: Grandpa and Grandma Green were raised in the Depression years when hard work and thrift were valued; the parents, Edith and Earl, came of age in the Summer of Love and married in 1978; and the younger generation, represented by cousin Jed Green (born 1969) and Edith and Earl's daughter Sun Green (born 1984), find their activist voices towards the end of the album.[25] The geography of Greendale, surrounded by the Pacific Ocean on one side and woodland on the other, is carefully mapped out on the fold-out album cover by the artist and former Young roadie James Mazzeo (who plays Earl in the *Greendale* film), together with further details of the town and its inhabitants in the liner notes, website and limited-edition book. The pencil drawing and sepia-coloured background give the town an old-time earthy feel, but the album also has a fable-like quality, upholding the values of family, community and nature in the face of capitalist forces. This is far from a bounded community. Many older family members have migrated from Idaho; some go mysteriously missing on journeys; and towards the end Sun Green embarks on an environmentalist journey to Alaska with the mysterious Earth Brown. The story is not entirely coherent though: themes and storylines drift in and out of focus, as if Young is not in full control of his fictional world or his characters' actions.[26]

The Green family displays a combination of conservative and liberal traits, with military service and community activism deeply ingrained in their history. Their peaceful lives are disturbed by Jed's arrest and imprisonment after he panics and shoots the local police officer Carmichael when his speeding car is found to contain cocaine and marijuana. This leads the media to descend on the Green household and links to a related story when corruption is discovered in the boardroom of the local corporation, PowerCo. Young explores the psychology of various characters over the course of ten tracks: sometimes the songs adopt a first-person perspective and at others we see the world more loosely from a character's point of view. Although the album charts the changes to the Greendale community over a broad timespan, the story draws continuities between generations: Grandpa's principled stand against media reporters after Jed's arrest leads to the old man's demise but also to the dawning of Sun's activism. Young takes the role of a critical commentator on 'Grandpa's Interview', suggesting that the old man's actions are heroic because he expresses the need for 'love and affection' (a sensibility that runs much deeper than just the late 1960s) and he seeks the right to be anonymous rather than being seduced by network news.

Jed's voice is the most slippery on the album because his troubled background is only hinted at: his father Stone Green fought in the Vietnam War and died in 1976 from a war-related illness; his mother committed suicide that same year; and Jed's younger brother Jacob died as a boy in a boating accident with his foster parents. Perhaps because Jed does not have a stake in the family he becomes a trickster figure and continues to participate in the drama of Greendale from inside his jail cell. Young's self-directed film adaptation of the album shows how Jed transforms into a freely roaming devil (he is more an everyday devil than an incarnation of evil) and heightens Sun's activism by bewitching Earth Brown to join her on the trip to Alaska.[27] Towards the end of the album and film Sun emerges as the central heroic character who takes forward the Green family legacy, while Jed fades into the background, carrying with him the hints of the supernaturalism in the Grateful Dead's 1970 song 'Friend of the Devil', where travel and mischief go hand in hand.

The final two tracks, 'Sun Green' and 'Be the Rain', are musically the most interesting on an album that some reviewers thought was marred by sludgy guitar playing. The *Washington Post*, for example, described the music as being 'as thin and meandering as its plot; nearly all the songs are just three chords of electric guitar, some humble bass notes and a bit of drowsy, mid-tempo drumming.' This is in contrast to the *New York Times* review of the album as a 'flower blossoming in the dirt', leaving the listener 'breathless with the beauty, hope, pathos and power of the music and the story'.[28] Most reviews fit between these two extremes. However, even though Sue Sorensen describes Young's message as one of 'compassionate and provocative patriotism' delivered in an 'unpolished' and 'ragged' style, critics rarely picked up on the fact that the Greens' moral anti-authoritarian community harks back to the early group experiments of the 1960s.[29] This sensibility is sharpened by the oppressive measures that the George W. Bush administration put in place after 9/11, as illustrated in the lyrics about surveillance paranoia on 'Leave the Driving'. This anti-authoritarianism also comes through strongly when Sun straps herself to a statue of an eagle in the offices of PowerCo and denounces a corrupt regime through a megaphone. Once Sun's activism is unleashed she openly attacks anything 'unjust or packed with lies'.

Her chief cause is an environmentalist one, stimulated by PowerCo's irresponsibility towards nature in order to enhance their profits. When Sun flees Greendale in 'Be the Rain' after her public stand (and on a charge of marijuana possession) it is not to abandon her community, but to tackle the root cause of environmental damage in the frozen wastes of Alaska. The nine-minute track is dominated by a chorus in which the singer rallies a community of activists to save Mother Earth by shouting through a megaphone about pollution and environmental destruction. It is also one of Young's most powerful travelling songs as the

driving guitar rhythm conveys the drama of Sun Green and
Earth Brown's outlaw run up the West Coast. The song's values
are distinctly New Age: they echo the Northern Lights imagery
of 'Pocahontas', but also the environmental sensitivity of older
Green family members that would not have been out of place in
the San Francisco of the late 1960s. Rather than a soft message of
peace and harmony, however, the harsh weather conditions and
the megaphone sound bites give the song a harder edge. For the
live performance on the 2003 tour the band was joined onstage
by Sun Green (played by Sarah White, a friend of Amber Young)
and a large cast of working characters, making this an exhilarating
counterpart to more delicate environmentalist tracks of the 1990s,
'Natural Beauty' and 'Mother Earth'.

These green and community causes were also mirrored in
Young's own life in the mid-1980s, at a time when he was being
criticized for drifting to the Right. In 1985 he co-founded the
charitable initiative Farm Aid, which revolved around an annual
concert that raised consciousness about the plight of American
farmers and contributed its proceeds to keep farming families
on their land. The Farm Aid concerts have left a powerful legacy
over 30 years, with the official Farm Aid song, 'The Last of His
Kind', closely echoing the *Old Ways* song 'Are there Any More
Real Cowboys?' in its elegy for hard work and sustained care
for the land. Young's collaboration with the Southerner Willie
Nelson and Midwesterner John Mellencamp (and later with New
Yorker Dave Matthews) means that Farm Aid cannot be associated
wholly with a Northern California sensibility or linked directly
to his adopted home. The long-running charity has nevertheless
benefited farmers in the central and valley regions of the state
that are often overlooked with the focus on the Pacific Coast.

A more local cause, which again has its roots in family, but
benefits the broader community of the Bay area, is Young's annual
Bridge School Benefit concert. These have taken place since 1986

in Mountain View, south of San Francisco in the heart of Silicon Valley. Inspired by Neil and Pegi Young's concerns about their son Ben's struggle with cerebral palsy as a young boy, the Bridge School, based in Hillsborough, has worked developmentally and collaboratively with a range of physical, cognitive and speech-related conditions since opening in 1987. The school offers specially designed education programmes for children between the ages of three and fourteen who have 'such severe communication and physical disabilities that they don't use speech to meet the majority of their communication needs'.[30]

The final chapter returns to the theme of augmented speech in Young's sonic experiments of the early 1980s, but it is clear that these two initiatives and the concerns of *Greendale* are informed by the communal values and experiences that Young encountered when he moved to the region in 1970. They balance his jaundiced view of what the hippie movement became with two very tangible activist causes that echo the early aspirations of the Grateful Dead to forge a moral community.

5 DREAM TRAVELLER

The cover of Young's 1975 album *Zuma*, based on a pencil
sketch by James Mazzeo, depicts a dreamlike California. Two
casually drawn figures fly from the snow-capped mountains
over a cactus-strewn desert towards the coast. A long-billed bird
of prey carries a naked woman in its claws, her outstretched
arms mirroring the angle of the bird's giant wingspan as
they fly together over a pyramid in the desert. A half-moon
rises amid the early evening stars as the hazy sun sinks to the
horizon. A ship is anchored near the shore. Its sails are at rest as
though it has just returned from a long voyage. Its masts form
two burial crosses, symbolizing death to balance the life-giving
luminescence of the moon.

Despite this dark imagery the overall mood is comically
exuberant, especially compared to the serious mythologies of
many 1970s progressive rock album covers and the melancholic
photograph of the musician looking out to sea on the cover of
On the Beach the previous year. Mazzeo's sketch might have
been a frame from a low-budget animation, if it was not for the
darkly etched border of 'Neil Young' and 'Crazy Horse' and the
four contrasting white letters of the album title that hover in
the sky. The drawing does not reflect the lyrics of *Zuma* with
any precision, but echoes the eclecticism of Young's music of the
mid-1970s, blending an affinity with the West Coast landscape
and imaginative journeys beyond the here and now.

Mazzeo sketched four versions of the cover image, based on a visual idea of Young's about time travel, a 'bird flying women over the desert, pyramids and stuff'.[1] Rather than the grand mythologies that fascinated prog rock bands, Mazzeo's image only provides a loose conceptual focus for the album.[2] There are visual echoes of the final two tracks – the Aztec temple in 'Cortez the Killer' and the shoreline of 'Through My Sails' – but the clearest reference point is to the second, seven-minute song 'Danger Bird'. The song's long, slow opening suggests that this mythological creature is just waking and preparing for a lengthy flight home. The bird is not as agile as he once was, but can still fly even though his wings have 'turned to stone'. We may be tempted to read the image of stone wings as a metaphor for Young's 'fossilized relationship' with Carrie Snodgress.[3] The song is both personal and epic, though, as the singer and bird soar above the dangerous city into a wind current that takes them homewards. The shadow imagery in the defiant closing lines of 'Danger Bird' echoes the final verse of 'Helpless', but here there are no colours to soften the experience – no lyrical 'yellow moon', no 'blue windows' – implying that this mythical flight is replayed in the singer's emotionally stark journey. This epic quality is amplified by Young's dramatic guitar, Billy Talbot's heavy bass, and counterpoint backing and lead vocals – even more so on the extended live version on the 1997 *Year of the Horse* album.

The *Zuma* cover and 'Danger Bird' are examples of dream imagery that punctuates Young's 1970s albums, often without clear lines separating sleeping from waking life. This shifting between layers of consciousness is animated via the flight of 'Danger Bird', the composition of which Young describes in visual terms: 'a series of pictures. You never see exactly the same thing. You go to new places.'[4] We might associate a fluid state of mind with drug and alcohol intake during the 1970s – the recording of *Tonight's the Night* was fuelled by tequila, Young ate marijuana-

A 1975 advertisement for the Neil Young and Crazy Horse album *Zuma*, including cover art by James Mazzeo.

infused honey slides during the making of *On the Beach*, and Crazy Horse reputedly took angel dust before recording 'Cortez the Killer' – but fluidity also emerges in a group of songs that explore the relationship between dreams and reality.

When he returned to dreams in the late 1980s, Young tended to signal their presence more explicitly, often harkening back to a particular time and place, such as the San Francisco of the late 1960s in 'Big Time' and 'Mansion on the Hill'. In these two songs reality is more stable than the all-enveloping 'dreamland' to which the singer awakes every morning in the *Tonight's the Night* ballad 'New Mama'. But even in later songs, such as the penultimate *Harvest Moon* track 'Dreamin' Man', Young recognizes that dreaming is both his problem and an imaginative resource that allows him to expand time and space. We might link this to the psychedelic scene of the late 1960s or to his live versions of The Beatles' 'A Day in the Life' in 2008–9, with its drug-induced daydream interlude. However, although his dreams might take him far from home, they have the capacity to reveal alternative cultures and expanded horizons. This tendency echoes the vision quests of many North American indigenous tribes, associated with states of heightened spiritual awareness experienced during a rites-of-passage journey, which taps into natural rhythms and tribal memories. Just as the vision of 'Danger Bird' allows Young to overcome his earlier hesitancy and to escape the tormenting city, so transformative dream imagery opens up emotional and imaginative worlds for him.

In exploring the relationship between travelling and dreams in Young's music and films this chapter moves beyond the geographical coordinates of the previous four. Dreams for Young are sometimes a puzzle to solve and at other times a new geography to explore, corresponding to the two dominant dream theories of the 1960s: the Freudian theory in which dreams are a working through of repressed psychic matter and the existential humanist view of dreams as an alternative topography. Dreaming is rarely a doorway to the state of lost innocence for which Young yearns in 'Sugar Mountain', but it has the capacity to transport the singer and the listener elsewhere. On this point, it is worth returning to the two concepts discussed in the introduction: drifting and turning. Through the act of dreaming Young can drift purposefully, pulling together sounds, images and colours in creative ways, and can explore the twists and turns of the unconscious where one image blurs with the next. The nature of dreams means that their shape keeps morphing. This can lead the dreamer towards deeper meaning, but can also drift away into impressions and noise. At times Young searches for direction – such as the quest on his 2007 track 'Spirit Road' to discover the 'long highway' within – and at other times escapes from meaning into a play of imagery and sound.

We can identify this second trend in one of Young's early dream songs, 'Broken Arrow'. This six-minute coda to the second Buffalo Springfield album *Buffalo Springfield Again* seems to be inspired by the early-summer release of The Beatles' concept album *Sgt. Pepper's Lonely Hearts Club Band*, leading Young to incorporate crowd noises from a Beatles concert and the opening distorted snippet of a live performance of 'Mr Soul', sung by drummer Dewey Martin. Despite its musical variety there is little input from the band, except for backing vocals by Richie Furay, added after Young had recorded the song in September 1967. Its power stems from Young's sound experiments and the visually arresting figure of a Native American standing alone on a riverbank with an empty quiver. This image of the 'vanishing Indian' with a broken arrow suggests either surrender to an unstoppable force or an offering of peace. What makes this a mysterious image is that there is no discernible enemy in sight; instead the verses describe a triad of social pressures (fame, adolescence and marriage) as if modern social organization has defeated the nobility of the Native American.

The question 'did you see him in the river?' incorporates the listener in a historical story in which nature is replaced by social ritual. This transition is reinforced by the river imagery, which seems more urban than rural and permits the figure no room to flourish. The complex phrasing that Young uses to describe the unarmed Native American is developed in the song's structure, where forward movement is interrupted by sound snippets: the burst of 'Take Me Out to the Ballgame' at the end of the first verse, the military drums in the second and the closing lounge jazz suggest that the Native American's voice is difficult to hear beneath layers of cultural sediment. But the subjects of each verse also find it hard to sustain their stories: the concert audience waits expectantly outside in the rain; the anxious adolescent 'hangs up his eyelids'; and the king and queen vanish in the midst of a wedding parade.[5] Each new scene takes us back to the haunting image of the Native American with his broken arrow; only the fade-out heartbeat suggests that his spirit survives in the face of debilitating modern forces.

The three parts of 'Broken Arrow' constitute probably the most formally arranged track of Young's career. More often he prefers to work fluidly with themes and sensations that meld into one another, as they do on another three-part song, 'Country Girl (Medley)', from CSNY's *Déjà Vu* album. Taking a more domestic subject as its focus, the song is nevertheless mythical. It links back to 'Broken Arrow' via the short song 'Down Down Down', which he had recorded with Buffalo Springfield but not released. This track has two moods: the first stems from the chorus of 'Broken Arrow', but with the enigmatic Native American replaced by a mysterious woman; the second mood stems from a set of unanswerable questions which Young revisits in 'Country Girl'. There are echoes of 'Nowadays Clancy Can't Even Sing' in the singer's frustrated attempt to see and think clearly, but here the questions cluster around the motives of the female figure who has committed a transgression that seems to require the singer's forgiveness. We have seen these elements before. The woman in the river is a similar kind of beckoning figure to the 'Cowgirl in the Sand' and arouses suspicions that she has been sharing her love around. But in 'Down Down Down' it seems as if the singer, too, has been unfaithful or has let her down. The lyric suggests equivalence between the two, but also confusion on behalf of the singer, particularly about the sequence of events, which words have meaning and who is most to blame.

The disorientation of 'Down Down Down' is lighter when it is recycled in the second part of 'Country Girl'. It is still a mazy song, though, introduced via the half-rhyme of the first couplet: 'Winding paths / through tables and glass'. The musical opening is drawn from 'Whiskey Boot Hill', a short orchestral piece that begins the second side of Young's debut album. In 'Country Girl' the piece is less dramatic and segues into the main theme of the song, where we see a dreamlike woman serving drinks at a celebrity bar. Just as 'Danger Bird' might be read biographically as referencing Young's split with Snodgress, so this waitress figure may be a reference to his first wife Susan Acevedo, even though the two were divorced by the time *Déjà Vu* was released. But 'Country Girl' transcends Young's biography and floats on a dreamlike plane. The song retains the theme of belatedness and the unanswerable questions, but then abandons confusion for an upbeat final section with harmonies by Crosby and Nash. There is again the sense of an indiscretion and fallen purity, but the early shattered images give way to rural courtship in the final verse as the singer finds an emotional clarity that the 'winding paths' of his dreams fail to deliver.

Young revisited dream imagery frequently in the late 1960s and 1970s, from the vision of the 'silver spaceships' seen from his basement prison on 'After the Gold Rush' to the uncertain haziness of 'Like a Hurricane', where the singer thinks he remembers once seeing his loved one in a 'crowded, hazy bar'. In both songs he manages to find transcendence within a dream world, perhaps inspired by the rural tranquillity he briefly experienced in Topanga Canyon in 1968–9 and then in La Honda from 1970. But there is often a groping for expression in this group of songs. We have seen in 'Tell Me Why' how the singer pushes himself to speak even though meaningful words do not come easily. Sometimes this inarticulacy seems like nervousness in the presence of a loved one and sometimes a deep incapacity that stops him from thinking and speaking clearly. It also links to Young's growing awareness that sound can often be a more meaningful medium of expression than lyrics. Slippery language can sometimes be an inspiration, sometimes a curse.

The eight-minute 'Like a Hurricane' is one of Young's best examples of musical transcendence. The bar transforms into the night sky, hovering between a poetic description of a music club and celestial imagery of light and stars. It is followed in the chorus by the song's central simile of a powerful storm which blows away the singer and envelops his attempts to express his love. The singer describes himself as 'just a dreamer' and his loved one as 'just a dream', the word 'just' suggesting that this 'foggy trip' is on the edge of reality, but also that this is a half-expression of a feeling that lies beyond words. The dreamy image of the woman blurs with the fantasies of his earlier songs, but he does not descend into wish fulfilment or sentimentality or hound-dog lonesomeness. Instead the swirling images become the focus of the song in his search for a quiet centre within the tumult. This tallies with Young's comment that he often sees 'a big blur of images' where one thing is 'seemingly unrelated' to another, explaining that 'if I see it and keep seeing it' the blur can sometimes return as 'a little glimmer of something'.[6] 'Like a Hurricane' locates these hints of understanding in a calm, sacred place, but the music moves in another direction when his driving lead guitar soars on the line 'getting blown away'. He uses this technique on other power tracks, such as his electrifying cover version of 'All along the Watchtower', which in its 'large dramatic gestures' is more reminiscent of Jimi Hendrix than Bob Dylan.[7] Young has acknowledged that the bridge into the chorus of 'Like a Hurricane' is inspired by Del Shannon's 1961 hit 'Runaway', before moving into the central guitar melody.[8] After the first chorus the intensity ebbs slightly ahead of the second verse, but the trance-like guitar solos that follow the second and third chorus are a fuller expression of his dreamscape than the lyrics, especially in live performances where the dream expands through extended solos.

If one set of dream images involves flying and strong natural forces, then another tendency is the search for authenticity in something basic and primitive. This most obviously links to Young's long-standing interest in Native American cultures that span the geography of the Americas: from First Nations tribes of Canada to South American indigenous groups. The movement of nomadic tribes across the plains of North America loosely reflects Young's own migratory journey and his shifting musical identity, from the persona of the 'Hollywood Indian' that he adopted in 1966–7 through to his onstage companion Woody, a wooden Native American to which he speaks on occasion, such as the April 2014 concerts at Dolby Theatre in Los Angeles, where Young treated Woody as a wise counsellor. We see the transformative imagery of the vision quest in some songs when time and space collapse into a moment of individual and collective insight, but in other songs he turns to native culture to lament a vanishing civilization, such as the isolated figure stuck between the river and the city in 'Broken Arrow'. This sense of being caught between worlds is expressed through a series of tensions: natural and urban, primitive and modern, north and south, technology and spontaneity, dreams and reality. Young's sympathies clearly lie with nature and the North, but for the other pairs it is not so easy to privilege one term over the other.

We see these creative tensions at play in one of Young's most popular Native American-themed compositions, his love song 'Pocahontas', written in 1977 but not released until *Rust Never*

Sleeps appeared two years later. The song begins with one of his most captivating images: the aurora borealis seen on an icy night. The singer either sees the Northern Lights from a remote vantage point, possibly Northern Manitoba or the Northwest Territories, or he imagines them in his mind's eye. The time and place of the song are unclear, although the canoes of the third line suggest we have been transported to an earlier time. This evokes the figure of Pocahontas, the Powhatan woman who legend suggests fell in love with the white settler John Smith in the early seventeenth century and had a child with the tobacco planter John Rolfe. The imagery also recalls the flight of Native Americans from European colonization and of violence perpetrated against tribal families. These disturbing images continue into the third verse, as the buffalo (a sacred animal and a symbol of preservation) is massacred during westward expansion. Young returned to this history on 'Peaceful Valley Boulevard', a song from 2010 which links the encroachment of the Transcontinental Railroad on the plains states in the 1860s to environmental danger 150 years later.

The turn occurs in the third verse of 'Pocahontas', when the image of the massacre wakens the singer from his dream world. Modernity is conjured in the shape of the taxis that flatten the singer's feet, but he manages to stay in touch with his ebbing reverie via the 'Indian rug' and ceremonial pipe. The last two verses can be seen as wish fulfilment in which Young imagines a life with Pocahontas. Given that the only written records of Chief Powhatan's daughter are by Virginian colonists, he might also be commenting on the legend as it has been transmitted into the twentieth century. This feels like his personal voice rather than an impersonation of John Rolfe or John Smith, but the pronouns are slippery, moving from his desire to be a trapper to a sense of collective loss. The vision of a 'homeland / we've never seen' could be interpreted either as a lost civilization or a destiny that has yet to be realized, as if Pocahontas and Young are fragments of the same mythical story.

This reflection carries through to the final verse, where the singer and Pocahontas are joined by the Hollywood actor and champion of Native American causes, Marlon Brando. Fresh from his role as Vito Corleone in *The Godfather*, Brando boycotted the Academy Awards in 1973 to protest the shabby treatment of Native Americans by film executives and sent the civil rights activist Sacheen Littlefeather in his place to collect his award for Best Actor. This unlikely but perfectly matched trio of Brando, Pocahontas and Young (European American, Native American and Canadian American) round out the song, as they chat on an imaginary campsite that seems to float across both time and space. Pocahontas is placed in the middle of the trio as a conduit between native and modern cultures, perhaps inspired by her marriage to an Englishman and her adoption of the anglicized name Rebecca. Young does not make explicit this symbol of racial mixing, but instead focuses on the futuristic 'astrodome' which exists in harmony with 'the first tepee', once again evoking the theme of time travel. That opening icy image contrasts with the campfire that warms the travellers as the reverie fades out with the trio engaged in conversation, before a final and solitary 'Pocahontas' echoes the 'borealis' that ends the first line.

The slipping between dreams and historical memory is exemplified in the penultimate track of *Zuma*, which brings together this interest in primitive cultures and the violent encroachment of the modern world. Often hailed as one of Neil Young and Crazy Horse's most mesmerizing guitar tracks, the seven-minute 'Cortez the Killer' revisits the historical encounter between the Aztec ruler Moctezuma II and the Spanish explorer Hernán Cortés during the Spanish colonization of Mexico. Despite its early sixteenth-century setting, the opening uses the present tense. We see Cortés 'dancing across the water' on his

Zuma-era Crazy Horse on Malibu Beach, photographed by Henry Diltz in 1975.

arrival in Mexico from Cuba, following Young's languid guitar
work of the opening three minutes, which, as one reviewer calls
it, 'drones, ebbs, and flows'.[9] Whereas we see the world through
Manson's hateful eyes in 'Revolution Blues', here Young adopts
the role of mythical storyteller, where violent conquest blends
with a dream world at a remove from historical reality. Cortés
isn't given a voice (not initially, at least) and his advancing army is
softened by the verb 'dancing' and in the consonance of 'galleons'
and 'guns'. The tension between the verb and nouns corresponds
with Young's claim that he wished to offer a balanced treatment
of the story: 'What "Cortez" represented to me is the explorer
with two sides, one benevolent, the other utterly ruthless.'[10] So
while the song can be seen to romanticize Aztec culture, it more
accurately deals with the binding of two civilizations, at a point
where European and Native American cultures fuse, particularly

as Cortés made alliances with various native groups on his march to the Aztec capital of Tenochtitlan.

Young claims that the song is based on 'a combination of imagination and knowledge'.[11] Disarmingly, though, he has also said that he did not know the myth very well and that he relied on patchy reading from his schooldays, quite possibly based on American historian Maurice Collis's account *Cortés and Montezuma* (1955).[12] The song skirts around details and reads more like a romance or a dream than a historically accurate retelling. It brushes over the topic of sacrifice, casually claims that 'war was never known' prior to the Spanish conquest, and avoids other issues such as Europeans bringing disease to the New World. Ulrich Adelt argues that the song quickly shifts from the story of Cortés and Moctezuma into an exploration of the singer's fantasy, without him 'even being aware of it'.[13] This reading suggests a lack of care on Young's behalf, especially as the song seems to be unfinished; some accounts suggest that the final verse was abandoned when the fuse on an amplifier blew.[14] But Adelt is perceptive in noting that the singer plays the role of both 'oppressor and victim', shifting between the perspectives of the Aztec ruler, the conquistador and the colonized people.[15] This plays out through a series of ambiguous images that could be either praising or damning. The multicoloured clothes worn by the Aztecs, for example, might symbolize pride in their cultural heritage or link to the gold that Moctezuma bestowed on the Spaniards to placate them on their arrival, based on the ruler's mistaken belief that Cortés was an embodiment of the avenging Mexican god Quetzalcoatl.

However we read the series of puzzling images, the singer appears to retreat from the historical scene in the final verse, where he reflects on a loved one and cannot understand how he lost her or his own path. This seems to support Adelt's reading that Young loses himself in his own fantasies, perhaps once again brooding about his split with Snodgress. However, it could equally be an example of Young impersonating another's voice. Here it could be Cortés reflecting on one of two women: Catalina Suárez, whom he married in Cuba and who later joined him in Mexico and died in mysterious circumstances; or, more likely, a Nahua woman named La Malinche, or Doña Marina, whom he met soon after landing on the east Mexican coast – she became his translator and they had a son, Martín, before the pair separated a few years after the conquest of Tenochtitlan. There are not enough clues to be sure who is speaking and who the woman is, but this reverie serves to humanize Cortés, before the fade-out returns to the violence of the song title. There is both certainty in the reverie and confusion about how the pair became separated. In this respect the song combines time travel with the logic of dreams in which memory, imagination and history zoom in and out of focus.

Young returned to Central and South America in the 1980s on 'Like an Inca' and 'Inca Queen' but they fail to replicate the grandeur of 'Cortez the Killer'. These tracks follow the theme of his 1978 song 'Ride My Llama', the lyrics of which reflect the llamas he keeps on his La Honda estate and his interest in historical and geographical journeys. In this latter respect, he links the Mexican attack of 1836 on the Alamo mission to travelling bareback from Peru to the Texas–Arkansas border town of Texarkana.[16] Unlike the hazy boundaries between dream and reality on 'Pocahontas' and 'Cortez the Killer', 'Ride My Llama' stays in the realm of fantasy. The song focuses on a troubadour from another planet who offers a mysterious gift – which one assumes is peyote, yage or marijuana – that helps the singer to telescope into his dream world. We might be critical of the politics of linking hallucinogenic drugs, outer space and South American culture, emphasized by the line 'as any primitive would' (a colonial term that is ideologically loaded when used to describe native cultures). But the fact that the song does not explicitly

mention drugs might mean the offering is a travel song or a totem
or the llama itself, often seen as a symbol of endurance that might
sustain the singer on his trip.

A more interesting revisiting of the past is to be found on
the near nine-minute track 'Goin' Home' on Young's album
Are You Passionate? (2002), with Booker T. & the MG's. The song
opens with General Custer's last stand at the Battle of the Little
Bighorn during the Great Sioux War of 1876, but the second
verse turns from the wind blowing through the bloody battlefield
to the musician feeling the same wind in his hair as he walks
downtown over a century later. The verbs of the third verse –
'weaving', 'cutting', 'slicing' and 'piling' – suggest that the wind
has intensified over time, but also that it can only be truly felt in
special moments of dream or vision. The second section deals
with bureaucracy and broken promises, before returning in the
final part to a historical image that strains against contemporary
life. A sophisticated female figure finds that 'a turn on a wooden
bridge' leads her into the battle scene, where she is surrounded by
thousands of warriors – presumably the three Native American
tribes that fought the U.S. Army at Little Bighorn. This imagery
is conjured up by a radio broadcast, but the 'battle drums' keep
pounding her car even when she switches the radio volume down.
The song ends with an image of transformation as the woman's
clothes change 'into sky and stars', as if she has been dragged into
a mythical story in which the celestial and terrestrial spheres are
part of a great pattern, only a portion of which can be seen and
understood. The simple repetition in the chorus of 'Goin' Home'
suggests that home does not exist in any one place. Just like the
distant homeland in 'Pocahontas', it can only be located via an
intersection of past and present and of dreams and reality.

Young's interest in Native American culture and historical
change is reflected in his composition for the Jim Jarmusch
film *Dead Man* (1995), at a time when he was between the sonic

experimentation of *Arc/Weld* and his collaboration with Pearl
Jam on *Mirror Ball*. Starring Johnny Depp as William Blake,
who transforms from a naive Midwestern accountant into a
frontiersman, bandit and Native American warrior, *Dead Man* is
often seen as a psychedelic Western that mines the iconography
of the Western film genre. Young's improvised music is as stark
and dramatic as Jarmusch's monochrome cinematography and as
mysterious as Blake's psychological and physical transformations.
Given that Jarmusch was listening to *Sleeps with Angels* while
thinking about *Dead Man*, it is tempting to find deeper resonances
between Young's music and particular features of the film, such as
the role of the enigmatic Native American drifter, Nobody (played
by the Cayuga actor Gary Farmer), the confusing terrain that
compounds Blake's existential bewilderment towards a place that
is also no place, and Blake's transformation into an in-between
figure who bridges the white Wild West and a vanishing Native
American culture (the choice of Depp might have been because
he claims Cherokee ancestry on his mother's side). But this would
be going too far. Young was not involved in the project until
Jarmusch had completed a 150-minute rough cut, and he agreed to
improvise the haunting score on electric guitar while viewing the
pre-production edit.[17]

   We have seen how nature and native cultures play out through
Young's dream and time-travel songs. These aspects also feature
in the final example of this chapter. One of the weirdest projects
of Young's career resulted in the 1982 release of his second film as
director, *Human Highway*, in collaboration with Dean Stockwell.
The film returns to the theme of apocalypse in Stockwell's
unmade film *After the Gold Rush*, but uses comedy, farce, slapstick
and surrealism to tell a story about the end of days. The new wave
band Devo play a group of space travellers who arrive at a post-
holocaustic earth where they find a rubble-filled landscape and a
deserted grey city, Linear Valley, somewhere in the southwest.

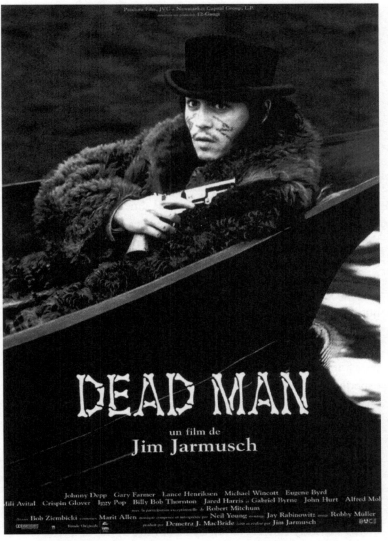

French promotional poster for *Dead Man* (dir. Jim Jarmusch, 1995), depicting Johnny Depp as William Blake on his river journey.

One of the travellers, played by Booji Boy (the persona of Devo's singer, Mark Mothersbaugh), makes his way through the rubble reciting a parody of Dylan's 'Blowin' in the Wind', in which the hope and expectancy of Dylan's song are replaced by futility and farce. We see the members of Devo glowing red as they work on a leaking nuclear reactor and sing 'It Takes a Worried Man', a highly processed version of the folk song 'Worried Man Blues', which becomes a surreal refrain through the film. The theme of apocalypse is interwoven with a more domestic story involving Young's character, the idiot mechanic Lionel Switch, who dreams of forming a rock band; Stockwell as Otto Quartz, the owner of a roadside diner and garage; and Dennis Hopper as the lazy and irritable chef Cracker. These three are surrounded by a cast of minor characters, including Pegi Morton as a mystery biker (filming started around the time that she and Young were married). Most of the film is a flashback to the day before the nuclear explosion in Cal-Neva, but the characters seem largely oblivious to the leaky reactor and impending holocaust.

The odd mixture of elements is partly because it took over four years to complete *Human Highway*, but the viewing experience is nevertheless a strange trip. The arrival of the Devo characters from outer space is not the only travel motif in the film. Among the actual and fantasy journeys is a powwow sequence, which involves a large wooden Native American figure which we have previously seen in the garage. The wooden figure provides a portal to a parallel universe where Lionel finds he is a famous rock star – a dream world he enters when knocked on the head while working underneath a car. The film cuts from Lionel's fantasy concert footage to a bonfire in the desert where the wooden figure is ritually burnt, along with similar icons, and where Lionel's rock-star alter ego and his entourage commune with a New Mexican tribe. Despite the disorienting use of

Neil Young and Dennis Hopper in Taos, New Mexico, on the set of *Human Highway* (dir. Neil Young and Dean Stockwell, 1982).

solarization, garish primary colours and overexposed shots, this is a reflective sequence accompanied by the wistful song 'Goin' Back', in which themes of renewal and disappearance converge. This brief moment of reflection about a place that is both present and absent is followed by the frenetic studio version of 'Hey Hey, My My', played by Young and Devo, in which the utopian and communal elements of the powwow break into sonic entropy. At the end of the song Lionel awakes from the dream, but he finds it difficult to distinguish fantasy from reality. This blurring carries through to a vaudeville reprise of 'It Takes a Worried Man', performed by the full cast of characters, before the nuclear reactor explodes and swallows the entire earth in a red glow.

The threatening image of the red sun that precedes the apocalypse in *Human Highway* returns us to the image of the setting sun on the cover of *Zuma*. As we have seen with *Prairie Wind* and *Greendale*, Young's cover imagery is often surprising if we look carefully, and *Zuma* is no different. James Mazzeo's images on the inner sleeve echo the visual elements of the cover, but in these alternate versions the flying companions have different features and proportions.[18] They travel from the coast towards the mountains on one side of the sleeve and to where the coast and mountains meet on the other. And on the back cover the flying duo hover near the ship, its sails once again at full mast in readiness for another journey. It is almost as if the dream world of *Zuma* replays itself, using the same psychic material in different combinations, where time and space morph in startling ways. This links to Young's admission in 1987 that his songwriting is not a rational process: 'my creation is not from a logical thought pattern; it's from a sub-dominant hemisphere of the brain. It's from another place. When I'm really writing, really playing, I'm not thinking at all.'[19] For these reasons, his music is frustrating if we try to establish an overarching perspective or a dominant image that can make sense of the whole. Instead, many of Young's songs offer momentary insights where reality makes sense, before drifting off again into dreamland.

6 SONIC JOURNEYS

Two tracks on Young's 2010 solo album *Le Noise* illustrate his interest in combining journey songs with musical experimentation. This was the first record without Crazy Horse to be dominated by electric guitar, and in order to generate an immersive sound Young recruited fellow Canadian Daniel Lanois as producer. Lanois' production work began in 1968 as a teenager and has since veered between acoustic and ambient tracks and more complex experiments with amplification. Working in this second mode on *Le Noise*, but respecting Young's dislike of overdubs, Lanois used a newly developed method of feeding back extracted sounds to enhance the themes of the album. The opening chord of the opening track 'Walk with Me', on which Young broods about lost travelling companions, is actually drawn from the middle, thereby creating a sonic loop that joins the living and the dead.

Lanois develops what he calls his 'black dub' technique further on the later *Le Noise* track 'Hitchhiker', which retells Young's migration story through the lens of drug-taking, generating a mood of premonition and aftermath that loops through the song. Lanois learned the dub technique from reggae production, based on a threefold method of extracting a chord or sound fragment, manipulating it and then reinserting it into the track. This method has an affinity with Young's own patchwork songwriting, especially because Lanois compares black dub to a dressmaker who fashions a 'beautiful dress and then takes the motif of the material, blows it up, cuts out a pocket and sticks it back on the dress. It's going to look like a different thing, but it's cut from the same cloth . . . it's not an addition, it's an expansion.'[1]

This, of course, was not the first time that Young had used a producer's signature sound to inflect the mood of an album. It had been a feature of *Neil Young*, his debut as a solo artist of 1968, in which Jack Nitzsche used overdubs to create a rich, orchestrated sound. Although Nitzsche's symphonic technique can also be heard on the Buffalo Springfield track 'Expecting to Fly', such was Young's dislike of the mix on the first pressing of *Neil Young* that he asked for a recall and reissue in 1969. He returned to orchestration on the *Harvest* tracks 'A Man Needs a Maid' and 'There's a World', and to add drama to his protest songs on *Living with War*, before returning to orchestral arrangements more systematically on *Storytone*. More often, though, he prefers deliberately rough production. This ragged sound does not mean that he neglects technicality, but the vocal clarity of *Storytone*, *Living with War* and *This Note's for You* is in large part down to his co-producer Niko Bolas. Lanois' patient mixing similarly gives the vocals extra depth on *Le Noise*, echoing the fuller vocals on Bob Dylan's *Oh Mercy* and *Time Out of Mind*, two albums produced by Lanois in 1989 and 1997 respectively. Lanois is very adept at musical tricks. 'Hitchhiker', for example, features Young's old electric guitar, his Gretsch White Falcon, which Lanois described as his 'big secret weapon': its two outputs allowed him to manipulate bass and treble through different amplifiers. The result is a sound that expands and envelops, but also startles. It doesn't permit the listener to settle into a comfortable response to music that explores the 'empty landscape' of darkness, even when love and devotion are its primary subjects.[2]

Young's sonic experiments are perhaps more instinctive than Lanois', but just as self-conscious. This stemmed from his teenage interest in creating live sounds and combining the guitar styles of his early heroes Randy Bachman and Hank Marvin. Jimmy McDonough notes that Marvin's addition of a whammy bar and Echoplex to his Fender Stratocaster and Bachman's improvised echo effects inspired the Canadian teenager to bend notes and to play around with echo.[3] Young is always reverential towards these early musical figures, including a pair of Southerners, Link Wray and Jimmy Reed: Wray taught him the versatility of the blues and how to control distortion and fuzz, such as on his brooding 1958 single 'Rumble', and from Reed he learned the advantage of using old harmonicas and guitars to produce a grooved sound. This led him to favour old instruments over newer models, including 'Old Black', his 1953 Gibson Les Paul Goldtop, the White Falcon and his Martin D-28 acoustic guitar, 'Hank'.

Although Young is sometimes dismissive of technical playing in favour of raw expression, the two cannot easily be separated. In an interview in *Guitar Player* in 1992, soon after he had toured with songs from *Ragged Glory* with Crazy Horse, he described his most-used equipment with relish: 'a tube Echoplex, an MXR analog delay, a Boss flanger, and an old white Fender reverb unit'.[4] The equipment means he is less reliant on his road crew to control effects and enables him to manipulate volume, tone, delay, echo and reverb onstage via a foot switch, 'the Whizzer', happy to hide bad notes and those he cannot play well in service to the whole sound of a song.[5] This sensory approach is technologically innovative but also more primal than the complex structures of progressive rock.

Young's interest in stretching sensory range echoes the immersive San Francisco psychedelic sound of the late 1960s, but also the way in which Jimi Hendrix shredded his guitar to expand the blues. There is also an element of the Grateful Dead here: Phil Lesh has discussed how natural and electronic sounds came together in the Dead's repertoire and allowed them to 'amplify the overtones to a degree never thought possible in an acoustic instrument'.[6] This does not subordinate live sound to studio experimentation where 'knobs and gauges' become the centrepiece, nor does it make composition into a wholly rational process. Instead, it enhances the instinctual elements of music.[7]

This ethos was also true for Hendrix, but in an even rawer fashion. This derived in part from the Seattle-born musician's self-taught style, in comparison to Lesh's formal training on violin and trumpet before he switched to bass on meeting Jerry Garcia in 1964. Hendrix's and Young's guitar styles could both be described as a stream of consciousness in which rises and falls, ebbs and flows, extensions and contractions, and trances and revelations become part of an organic rhythm that does not easily break into distinct sequences. Young learned a mood of dramatic expectation from Hendrix, creating a pulsing forward movement even as it loops back to an earlier point. Albin Zak describes Young's search in the mid-1970s for a floating, elevated sound as heroic, based on a performance style that became increasingly muscular in the early 1990s.[8] Young has always been a physical musician, but more so after he took up weights and regular exercise to combat post-polio fatigue in the mid-1980s. Muscle gain contributed to increased power on *Freedom* and *Ragged Glory* and led him to compare his live guitar playing to projecting a missile.[9] This did not mean he gave up his light touch. The Hispanic-influenced 'Eldorado' on *Freedom* is a great example of the musical storyteller weaving his way through a variety of moods, while the extended guitar break in the middle of 'Change Your Mind', filmed live for Jonathan Demme's *Complex Sessions* (1994), is a masterclass of Young switching seamlessly between lurching his whole body into powerful guitar chords and then pulling back into a gentler, dreamlike groove.

Hendrix's style has been a continuing influence on Young and links closely to an immersive, psychedelic sound.[10]

Neil Young playing 'Old Black' (and wearing an Elvis T-shirt) in concert with Crazy Horse, Desert Sky Pavilion, Phoenix, Arizona, April 1991.

Sheila Whiteley breaks this into a number of elements: the manipulation of timbres, an upward movement, lurching and oscillating harmonies, a mixture of even and uneven rhythms, and sound collages.[11] Layering sometimes draws the listener towards overarching meaning and sometimes escapes from meaning into noise, where music variously breaks down, starts up, stretches out and moves in multiple directions – in sequence and at times simultaneously.

Young's colour imagery from the mid-1960s is also expressive of his sound palette, particularly as colours often bleed together or cannot easily be resolved into one or another. This technique can be compared to Hendrix's 1967 track 'Love or Confusion' with its focus on colours 'without names' and 'without sounds', suggesting that psychedelic blues moves around a point of concentration without ever resting on a fixed centre. On occasions this sense of disorientation is explicit: both 'Love or Confusion' and Young's 1969 song 'Round and Round (It won't be Long)' picture the descending circle as a movement into a dark space where it is hard to retain a stable identity. Given that Young is often preoccupied with trying to break into flight, this descent suggests a musical attachment to the earth. Sometimes this is enabling (such as on the strident 2012 track 'Walk Like a Giant', which ends with over four minutes of thudding giant steps) and sometimes it prevents the individual from being creative ('Transformer Man' from 1982 is an attempt to throw off the earthly shackles of a physical and developmental disability).[12]

Hendrix did not just rely on instinct but had a number of self-conscious guitar tricks, including reverb, echo and phasing (often stemming from a fuzz effect or grinding sound achieved by pulling down the whammy bar), and he deliberately moved between octave doubling (using a special device, 'the octavia') and octave dividing (unamplified except for a microphone). Young learned from Hendrix how to drive forward while drifting around chords, as he does on the live album *Weld* (1991). This meandering style that varies the accent on notes can be compared to 'a state of tripping' or a 'psychedelic calliope-like effect'.[13] Both descriptions suggest a mode of sonic travelling that resonates with many of Young's lyrics and nuances the elevated sound that he describes in his *Guitar Player* interview.

We can hear Hendrix clearly on Young's electrified version of 'All along the Watchtower' at the 1992 Dylan anniversary concert, and in his even heavier rendition of the song with Pearl Jam in 2004, but he often blends Hendrix's histrionic style with other borrowed elements. For example, his cover of Dylan's 'Blowin' in the Wind' on the *Weld* tour begins with the noise of warfare and an anthemic guitar reminiscent of Hendrix's rendition of 'The Star Spangled Banner' at the Woodstock Festival. And, perhaps taking inspiration from Hendrix's electrified version of 'Sgt. Pepper's Lonely Hearts Club Band' at the Royal Albert Hall in November 1967, the coda to Young's version of 'A Day in the Life' on his summer 2009 European tour also evokes the bluesman. The last three minutes of The Beatles' song at the Glastonbury Festival on 26 June were full of guitar noise, before closing with a few solemn notes on glockenspiel; and at the end of the 23 June concert in Nottingham he left the stage with his untuned and flailing guitar strings reverberating through the amp. Whereas Hendrix set light to his guitar and Pete Townsend of The Who smashed his guitar onstage as theatrical acts of nihilism, Young respects his instruments. At the Nottingham concert Old Black was left propped up in stately fashion as the amplified distortions faded out. The technique corresponds to what William Echard calls 'just breaking-up' distortion; we often hear 'the continual buzz of decaying guitar notes' in his songs with Crazy Horse and he preserves the integrity and the colour tones of his music even when he bends chords.[14]

This does not mean he is shy of taking instruments beyond their natural sonic range. His interest in extremes is dramatized in the surreal twelve-minute version of 'Hey Hey, My My (Into the Black)', performed with Devo for the film *Human Highway*. The repetitive groove of the three overdriven guitars seems to have a reactive effect on Booji Boy's keyboard, which starts to feed back and eventually breaks down into a cacophony. In the song's final phase Young brings his guitar into close proximity with the cot in which Booji Boy plays his keyboard. He rocks the cot back and forth, before reaching over to turn the knobs and faders on the synthesizer, hastening the coda where the guitars give way to pure keyboard feedback. This anarchic spirit might have stemmed from Devo's founding idea of 'de-evolution', but Young clearly relished the opportunity to turn guitar rock on its head.[15] Here repetition, distortion and noise replace the melodic riffs, synchronicity and progression that characterized 1970s rock. Had *Human Highway* been released in 1978 this performance would have probably been hailed as more radical. Although the punk attitude, fast angular guitars and keyboard cacophony still felt fresh when the film was finally released in 1982, it fell in the shadow of other new wave, No Wave and electro bands, rather than leading the way in sonic experimentation.

Young did not save all his experiments for side projects like *Human Highway*. Following the raw guitar sound of *Re-ac-tor* in 1981, his interest in developing the electric range of Crazy Horse led a decade later to the release of *Arc/Weld*. *Weld* offers a heavier rendition of extended guitar tracks from *Ragged Glory*, where the muscular instrumental sections overtake the lyrics as the focal point. This is even more apparent on the 35-minute sound collage *Arc*, which stretches and distorts fragments from 'Like a Hurricane' and 'Love and Only Love' until they are barely recognizable, except for the first two lines of 'Like a Hurricane' that fade in and out of the song. *Arc* was influenced by Sonic Youth, his opening act on the Ragged Glory tour with which he detected strong musical synergies.[16] On *Arc* he deliberately collapsed boundaries and dispensed with rhythm in order to create 'molten' music that does not rest in any one place; the result, he hoped, 'just keeps changing all the time . . . it's completely free'.[17] He wanted a form that both progresses (circling around 37 sound pieces extracted from previous songs) and degenerates at the same time: 'by the time you get to the end, it's a little more frantic, a little more out of touch', he said, it's starting to lose its mind a little.'[18] This blurring of musical boundaries is mirrored in the grainy footage Young took of the 1987 Crazy Horse tour. This footage was intended for a lo-fi film, *Muddy Track*, with an emphasis on noise and distortion, but it remained unreleased until some extracts were included in Jim Jarmusch's *Year of the Horse*. Produced as a live album and documentary in 1997, Jarmusch's camera follows the Crazy Horse tour of the previous year through concert footage and garage-style interviews. The aim was to dispense with the pretence of rock in order to capture the energy and grungy improvisation of the band's live sound.

Young's collaboration with Pearl Jam in the mid-1990s offered another direction for stretching his guitar style. Given that Young was dubbed 'the godfather of grunge' in late 1991; Sonic Youth, Dinosaur Jr and The Flaming Lips all contributed to 1989's *The Bridge* tribute album, and Kurt Cobain quoted a line from 'Hey Hey, My My' in his suicide note of April 1994, it was not so surprising that a year later Young recorded with probably the most commercial of the West Coast grunge bands, Pearl Jam.[19] *Mirror Ball* is the only album they made together, but their collaboration has been long-lasting: Pearl Jam played 'Rockin' in the Free World' a number of times with Young in 1993 and the band appeared frequently at Bridge School Benefit concerts, including a powerful acoustic rendition of 'Walk with Me' with Young in 2010, included on the *Pearl Jam Twenty* album.

Jimmy McDonough is scathing of the collaboration, comparing it to the media hype of Young joining CSN.[20] An article from a 1995 issue of NME is more positive, suggesting that Young and Pearl Jam worked together on *Mirror Ball* to come to terms with the shared trauma of Cobain's suicide. This piece suggests that the Seattle group was drawn to Young's survival instinct, while Young was hooked by Pearl Jam's 'big machine' and their shift beyond the cynicism of grunge.[21] *Mirror Ball* is an unremarkable album, though, perhaps because it was recorded in four days. The playing echoes the dirty guitars of Crazy Horse, but often without a compelling underpinning rhythm. The five-minute 'Downtown' is the standout track, where the lyrics picture Jimi Hendrix playing in the back room and Led Zeppelin onstage (Young had played guitar with Jimmy Page for a rendition of 'When the Levee Breaks' in 1995), but the lyrics seem sloppy even when they address the tricky issue of abortion. Of greater interest is Pearl Jam's two-track single 'Merkin Ball', drawn from the same sessions, with Young on guitar and organ. The single's cover image of a wrecking ball smashing against a ruined building distorts the celestial iconography of *Mirror Ball* and reveals a nihilistic undertow to the collaboration.

The association with the grunge movement reveals a different West Coast alliance to the folk-rock fraternity from which Young had tried to distance himself in the second half of the 1980s. It also harks back to his shift away from the smoothness of *Harvest* in the early 1970s towards a deliberately ragged sound. Young's admission that he headed towards the ditch after the commercial success of *Harvest* affected both the score and the lyrics of *Time Fades Away* and *Tonight's the Night*. Not only are they rawer than his previous two albums (most of *Tonight's the Night* was recorded in a single day, on 26 August 1973), but also the elements of discord and disintegration that we see in more exaggerated form in his later guitar experiments are here built into his vocal delivery. This is most obvious in his straining to hit the high key of the quiet tracks 'Mellow My Mind' and 'New Mama'. The power of these songs derives from the unusual combination of drifting and angst, punctuated by a darker sense of nihilism. On 'Borrowed Tune', for example, the singer climbs a ladder with his head 'in the clouds'. This might be a symbol of transcendence or an astral search for Bruce Berry, but there is equally a sense that the climb takes him nowhere meaningful.

These elements only add to the discordancy of the two versions of 'Tonight's the Night'. William Echard notes that the recording of the title track was fuelled by drinking and drugs during a ramshackle wake for Bruce Berry, the roadie whose heroin overdose of June 1973 is relived in the title track, and Crazy Horse guitarist Danny Whitten, who suffered a similar fate eight months before (we hear Whitten singing on 'Come On Baby Let's Go Downtown', recorded three years earlier). The result is bleak and disturbing, not least because it contains 'a level of emotional distress foreign to most rock music' of the time.[22] This mood led Young to develop an alter ego based on a darker version of himself, as seen in the spectral figure on the album cover and his idiosyncratic behaviour on the 1973 Tonight's the Night Club Tour, when it seemed that he was heading for the same fate as Whitten and Berry. It also tallies with Young's comment that the record was 'the most liquid album I've ever made' and that it is 'like an OD letter . . . about life, dope and death'.[23]

The impulse towards disintegration is not just embodied in his ditch trilogy but came through strongly in the late 1970s. Young spoke about it in 1990 in his audacious comment that 'my whole career is based on systematic destruction . . . You destroy what you did before and you're free to carry on.'[24] It can also be heard on *Rust Never Sleeps*, in the cacophony of 'Welfare Mothers' and 'Sedan Delivery' and in the reckless anarchism of 'Hey Hey, My My', which, as we have seen, also marks his collaboration with Devo on *Human Highway*. The pantomime child persona of Booji Boy can be seen as a more self-consciously theatrical version of the trickster figure that Young adopted for *Tonight's the Night*, and which later resurfaced in Jed Green's transformation into the mischievous devil on *Greendale*. Young wore a Sex Pistols T-shirt for the film version of 'Hey Hey, My My'and adopted a badass, punk attitude, while Devo's edgy and anarchic elements come through strongly as Booji Boy intones barely comprehensible lyrics in a voice midway between an infant and a computer. The song is trancelike and disintegrative; its repetitive rhythm is too much for the tight studio space and leads to system overload as the intensity breaks down the physical structure of Booji Boy's cot.

Young is too varied an artist to inhabit a particular musical trajectory for very long. Even in the apocalyptic elements of 'Hey Hey, My My' (foreshadowing the actual apocalypse at the end of *Human Highway*) we see the seeds of a more progressive theme: an interest in alternative forms of communication and augmented speech. In part this stemmed from developments in musical technology in the late 1970s, such as the digital sampling synthesizer and the vocoder, which opened up new possibilities for playing and recording: the German electronic band Kraftwerk, for example, started using the vocoder in the early 1970s, with increasing recognition after *Trans-Europe Express* and *Man Machine* in 1977–8. But the preoccupation with communication mainly derived from Young's personal life, when in 1979 he and Pegi found that their son Ben had a severe form of cerebral palsy – a congenital condition that his first son Zeke experienced in milder form. Given that Ben could not easily speak due to a high degree of muscular spasticity from birth and very limited coordination, his parents worked hard with him on alternatives to vocal articulation.

The embodiment of this can be heard on what is probably Young's most surprising record. His 1982 release *Trans* is another patchwork album, containing straightforward songs such as the opening 'Little Thing Called Love', a reprocessed version of his early song 'Mr Soul', and a number of electronic tracks – 'Computer Age', 'We R in Control', 'Transformer Man' and 'Sample and Hold' – that represent a sharp U-turn in his output, arriving on the back of his previous album, the trudging *Re-ac-tor*. *Trans* certainly cannot be dismissed as a throwaway record or merely a rebuke to the Geffen label to which Young had signed (unhappily) earlier that year.[25] The album cover revisits the familiar 'nature versus city' theme via two contrasting images of cars and hitchhikers: on the right we see a conventional hitchhiker against a backdrop of firs trying to flag down a retreating 1958 Cadillac, while on the left a computerized cyborg raises an expectant hand towards a futuristic electric car with headlights ablaze. Light and movement push our attention towards the left; we see a jet overhead and the bright headlights of another car or a power station in the background. If there is a critique encoded in Barry Jackson's cover image (foreshadowing his imaginative automobile artwork for ZZ Top's *Afterburner* and *Recycler* covers) then it is flagged only subtly: the image tilts diagonally on an axis, as the bright, computerized urban world on the left weighs down the darker natural images on the right.

This swallowing of nature can be heard on the electronic tracks of *Trans*, on which cyborgs and computers win out over the natural world that Young had celebrated only a few years earlier and to which he soon returned on *Old Ways*. The prominence of Kraftwerk's favourite vocoder, the Sennheiser VSM201, is the most obvious element, but so too is the innovative use of Nils Lofgren as a member of the Trans Band. As captured on film for the Live in Berlin concert of October 1982, Lofgren becomes a man-machine on the stage and responds theatrically to Young's processed commands. At times Lofgren seems to be a puppet with little or no autonomy, but he gives the performance an emotional intensity that Young argued, somewhat paradoxically, was closely linked to computers.[26]

Despite this musical departure and the bewilderment of audiences that witnessed the *Trans* tour, Young did not abandon the autobiographical mode entirely, or dedicate himself to electronic machinery in the robotic manner of Kraftwerk. 'Transformer Man' is the most personal of the album tracks, exploring the ways in which computers generated expressive possibilities for his son. The song's themes are both worldly and celestial, but the focus is on a computerized realm; a push-button allows the central figure to gain mastery over his environment without erasing the human centre of the song, as expressed through the images of shining and electrifying eyes. This journey is again both personal and epic. The transformer turns a disabling condition into one where agency is possible – as revealed on the back-cover image: a cross-section of a fully functioning heart, but with circuitry added.

The theme of augmented life is taken much further in 'Computer Age' and 'Sample and Hold', where the vocodered vocals explore a transformed world. This operates on a sonic rather than a linguistic level as the lyrics are almost impossible to decipher without the song sheet to hand. The title 'Sample and Hold' and the refrain 'a new design, new design' are the song's audible mantras. Most often the voice blurs into the high treble of a song that lacks the positive metamorphosis of 'Transformer Man' in favour of a futuristic world in which hair, eyes, weight, disposition and mood are all digitally encoded. 'Sample and Hold' shares a critique of consumerism with a number of early 1980s electronic groups (and pre-dates by a decade U2's parody of late capitalism on their Zoo TV tour of 1993), picturing a cultural system in which consumer perfection feels like it could be a reality.

The song turns biology into a series of electronic codes which are embodied in the tinny synthesizers that dominate the track. The processed vocal moves between the top-end in the chorus (as if a vestige of humanity lurks within the system) to a bassier

Trans (1982) cover designed by Barry Jackson, depicting a clash between the natural world and a futuristic cityscape.

robotic voice in the verses (as if the natural energy has been subsumed into computer hardware). Young's human voice fades in and out during the five minutes of a track which seems strangely organic given the repetitive rhythm, perhaps because it retains a compelling melody. The 'we' of the song seems relatively benign in the claim to deliver genetic perfection, but it takes on a darker, Cold War hue in 'We R in Control', linking political power ('chief of staff', 'think tanks') to a destabilizing influence over nature and culture ('the flow of air', 'the TV sky'). That the lyrics are virtually indecipherable means that the critique is partially submerged under the wash of electronic music. But this does not lessen the impact. Young understood that there were fewer easy exits from the lures of late capitalism than there had been in the 1970s.

This departure was not just that of a former hippie waking up to a new world of personal computers, synthesizers and MTV, but a musician who was both genuinely excited but also worried by a computerized future. It is less the machines or processes themselves, and more how they can be manipulated by agents of power that disturbs the record. Lurking at the centre, and in the album title, is the transformer man who both reclaims agency for his son and recalls the struggle that Young himself underwent as a boy and young man in his battle with polio and epilepsy. He revived the images of physical jerkiness and fragmentation on 'Mr Soul', when he rerecorded the song for *Trans* with an electronic score – images that link to a child who needs machinery to augment his physical and developmental disability.

Young's songs of the time are littered with images of movement, such as a track he performed live only once in 1982, 'After Berlin', which compares the singer to a child 'running down the road' but needing help on the way. Such images are often augmented ones as he worked through the implications of Ben's difficulty to communicate. The emphasis on the struggle to speak recalls the frail voice and lack of confidence of Young's late-1960s music, which George McKay describes as 'quivering and shaking, uncertain and liable to break down'.[27] But here, as William Echard discerns, the distinction between the biological and the cybernetic begins to collapse.[28] Young recognized that computers are no panacea, but they can help when harnessed to a combination of imagination and hard work.

We might read the drifting elements of his songs as symptomatic either of his migration from Canada to California or of deep biological and neurological impulses that lend unpredictability to his compositions. Either way, this drift

Neil Young and Nils Lofgren play with the Trans band in Saint-Germain-des-Prés, Paris, September 1982.

suggests a hovering between psychological states that can be traced back to a combination of different guitar styles among his early musical heroes and to the dynamic transitions of Hendrix. His sonic journeys loop around each other, in much the same way as the imagery of his early songs rarely settles on a distinct colour field. We also see this in his vocoder experiments in which human and electronic voices overlap as he searches for an alternative channel that can emotionally connect with his son. Although *Trans* is an anomaly – he has never dedicated an album to electronic music since (despite using it in piecemeal ways on *Landing on Water* and *Life*) – it shares some formal

145

qualities with the heavier sound of Crazy Horse. Whatever the mode, Young rarely loses sight of emotional connectedness, exemplified by the rearranged but still recognizable fragments of 'Like a Hurricane' on *Arc*. There is a more conventional side to this too. The emphasis on acoustic performance at the Bridge School Benefit concerts reveals his belief that stripped-back music has the potential to reach across the divide of cognitive and developmental disability in a more basic way than electric or electronic music can.

What emerges from this matrix of musical sounds is a constant shuttling between styles and directions that does not allow him to settle in one place for long. There is an avant-garde impulse here as he keeps changing his line of attack, but Young has remained within the mainstream of folk, country and rock while still carving a space where he can experiment with and blur genres. Returning to old collaborators – whether it is CSN, Crazy Horse, Jonathan Demme or Jim Jarmusch – has enabled him to both move on and circle back, ensuring that an old sound is never lost but can be reworked in new ways. Like the rapid turnover of members of his first serious band The Squires, Young has often picked up musical companions along the way. However, apart from the odd exception, like pedal-steel guitarist Ben Keith, he rarely takes these fellow travellers consistently from one project to the next. When he sings on 'Walk with Me' 'I lost some people I was traveling with', he is thinking of Keith and film collaborator Larry Johnson, both of whom died earlier in 2010, but he finds walking alone is as valuable as taking companions with him. This is one reason that his soundscapes change so frequently; another is his habit of abandoning projects and then later reviving songs, leading to a number of albums with ragged and contrasting edges.

We have seen Young in this chapter veer towards lo-fi, grunge, discord and amplified distortion, but there is nearly always an element of control among all this drift. His musical

Photograph of Pono and vinyl of Neil Young, *Decade* (1977).

turns are sometimes surprising and his travels sometimes seem
to lack direction, but there is an art to his apparent artlessness
and a willingness to return to abandoned or unfinished songs.
Despite his critique of a computerized world in *Trans*, Young
respects musical technology, but only when it does not flatten
music. His long-standing project to manufacture Pono, a
portable, high-quality digital music device, is testament to
this. Pono was designed as a superior download service to rival
MP3 players and Apple's iPods. These devices might dazzle the
consumer with their high-tech urbane design (to recall the
Situationist Guy Debord's warning) but, according to Young's
research, they are only capable of delivering 5 per cent of the
original sound quality. Downloading has made music more
accessible, but Young believes it has lost its musical essence by
becoming commodified content with reduced audio quality, as
he expresses in the lyrics of 'Driftin' Back'. He compares MP3
audio to listening to music underwater, whereas his aspiration for
Pono (or PureTone, as it was originally conceived) is for listeners
to download music in a form that preserves the quality of the

studio recording.[29] He couches this in terms of technological improvement and a moral and spiritual quest for an idealized sound, which can also be seen as an ongoing search for a musical home: 'the spirituality and soul of music is truly found when the sound engulfs you . . . and your senses open up allowing you to feel the deep emotion in the music.'[30]

After three years of planning and a very public fundraising campaign announced at the South by Southwest (sxsw) music festival in March 2014 (in which investors were promised early-release devices in return for a Kickstarter payment), Pono was finally launched in mid-October 2014 at the Dreamforce information technology conference, held in San Francisco. This commercial venture is a new departure for Young and has led to scepticism that he was just trading on his fame.[31] But the attempt to rescue something that has been lost – using lossless FLAC files rather than compressed MP3 files to preserve the original recorded sound – recurs through his career, chiming with Jack White's emphasis on more truthful recording techniques to combat substandard replicas.[32] There is an element of nostalgia in Young's emphasis on communal musical experience (the system facilitates this via a digital ecosystem, Pono World, and a 'community cloud' of listeners) and in his comparison of true sound to valleys and mountains in contrast to the flat deserts of MP3.[33] This nostalgia can also be heard in his song choice and use of Jack White's 1940s Voice-O-Graph booth for the recording of *A Letter Home*. But there is also an equal willingness to embrace technology to preserve musical quality in the face of a digital industry geared up to instant access.

Young's drifting between different soundscapes does not mean either that his projects lack direction or that his quest for a musical home is a futile one. It is just that these soundscapes cannot be lined up neatly to create a linear journey leading to a fixed destination. Instead, as we have seen, his sonic travels are full of sharp bends, turnings back, embracing and then abandoning new technologies, collaborating with others and then pressing on alone. Just as his environmental interest in ecosystems comes to the fore on his 2014 album *Storytone*, so over the course of his career he has emphasized the complex interconnections between organic and mediated sounds and between playing and listening.

CONCLUSION: HUMAN HIGHWAY

In late May 1973, just as the Senate Watergate Committee was stepping up its hearings into high political corruption, Young joined up with Crosby, Stills and Nash in Hawaii to write and rehearse what would have been their third album together. Young rented a boathouse in Mala Wharf on the island of Maui while Crosby moored his own boat, *Mayan*, nearby. He and Nash had just come from providing backing vocals for Young's *Time Fades Away* tour and the foursome began the project with a renewed sense of purpose, emerging out of what Nash called 'a giant fog of psychic and musical connections' between them.[1] There was room in the boathouse for family, partners and manager Elliot Roberts. They worked harmoniously and Nash's friend took a great cover shot of the band on the coast: Young looks tanned and relaxed, wearing a bandana over his shoulder-length hair, shorts and an open plaid shirt.[2]

CSNY planned to record the album, to be titled *Human Highway*, back in La Honda. However, when they reconvened a fortnight later the holiday feelings had evaporated and the Pacific sun had set on the project. Nash believes that drugs came between them towards the end of the Hawaiian trip, particularly Stills's cocaine habit, and on his return to California Young was deeply affected by the news that his roadie Bruce Berry had overdosed in Los Angeles on 7 June.[3] Whatever the reasons for the ill-feeling during the recording session, the album was abandoned with only a few songs recorded, including 'Human Highway', which Young released as a solo version five years later on *Comes a Time*.

Although the album was never finished, a number of tracks, including 'Human Highway' and 'Hawaiian Sunrise', were included a year later in the set lists of the 1974 CSNY summer tour. When the tour started on 9 July in Seattle Center Coliseum, President Nixon was close to resigning and Young had adopted a new look – short hair and aviator glasses – following his strange stage behaviour on the Tonight's the Night Club Tour the previous autumn when he seemed to have spun into an alter ego, triggered by the deaths of Danny Whitten and Bruce Berry. Crosby was negative about the size of the stadia that CSNY played and grumbled that the stage was too far away from the audience.[4] He even dubbed the series of 31 concerts 'The Doom Tour', perhaps due to the effects of cocaine, although footage from Landover, Maryland and London (included in the CSNY 1974 box set) profiles the repertoire of a band that could still get it together despite interpersonal tensions.

All four were exhausted when the tour drew to a close on 14 September at London's Wembley Stadium, but they decided to give their recording project another go, this time in Sausalito across the Golden Gate Bridge from San Francisco. The studio arguments began almost straightaway and, according to Crosby, Young left one day saying '"Well, see you guys tomorrow." And he never came back.'[5] Young's leave-taking has become almost as mythologized as his departure midway through the ill-tempered Stills/Young Band tour in the summer of 1976, on the heels of another failed CSNY recording session in Miami. After playing nineteen shows together, Young sent Stills a telegram saying, 'Dear Stephen. Funny how some things that start spontaneously, end that way. Eat a peach. Neil.'[6] Although CSNY played and recorded periodically from the mid-1980s (including a ramshackle two-song performance at the Live Aid concert in July 1985), the creative energy of 1973–4 never returned.

We might interpret this as an aspect of Young's enigma as a 'loner' or his ability to 'walk on' when creativity turns sour (to cite two of his song titles), or as part of his journey from road to ditch which he undertook after the success of *Harvest*. When asked about this second abandoned studio session in 1975 in a *Rolling Stone* interview with Cameron Crowe, Young mentioned weariness, the imminent birth of Crosby's daughter and the difficulty of reconciling four strong viewpoints. In truth, the non-recording of *Human Highway* was just one of a number of album projects in the 1970s that Young did not complete as originally planned. What the abandoned *Homegrown*, *Chrome Dreams* and *Oceanside–Countryside* sessions produced was a diverse range of songs that ended up scattered through later studio and live albums. We have seen in previous chapters that not only do travel and movement permeate Young's lyrics, but also his songs themselves drift in unforeseen and surprising ways, often appearing as part of a different project or in an alternative form.

'Human Highway' is a good example of this. Finally released on *Comes a Time* with backing vocals by Nicolette Larson, the song explores the long-standing tension in Young's music between nature and the built environment. Coming down to join the 'human highway' from the calm of the 'misty mountain' (perhaps a cross between Topanga Canyon and the Canadian Rockies) suggests trading in hippie-style drifting for a purposeful journey towards a destination. The highway is certainly more linear than the 'twisted road' with which the book began. But his path appears less bewildering in the mountain mists than it does within a busy world of institutional relationships, industry pressures and personal rivalries, suggesting that the sensory delights of nature vanish in the rush of traffic. This is not an anti-urban song, or a rejection of modern travel – far from it, given his lifelong love of transportation and driving. What it suggests is that the pastoral renewal that characterizes other tracks on *Comes a Time* and *Harvest Moon* struggles to survive the speed and pollution of contemporary life.

Importantly, the highway is not a monolith for Young. On the track 'Interstate' (1990), for example, it is a lonely road that keeps alive the prospect of taking his guitar home; and on the slow-paced 'Roger and Out' from *Living with War*, the 'hippie highway' is a metaphor for life where drifting and transformations converge. 'Roger and Out' is about the loss of a travelling companion and a nation that has lost its way, mired in a new war in the Middle East that revived the spectre of the drawn-out conflict in Vietnam. Released for Veterans Day in 2006, the video is full of war imagery. Photographs of the highway dissolve into combat footage of the Vietnam War, while scrolling statistics convey the monthly U.S. death toll in Iraq since the initial strike of March 2003. The final shots illustrate the ways in which personal and national stories often fuse in his songs: we see the light going down on the moving highway as a solitary individual contemplates the list of dead soldiers inscribed on the Vietnam Veterans Memorial in Washington, DC.

While Young is often keen to inhabit the misty mountain where he can explore sensory and emotional relationships at his leisure, he periodically takes his place on the human highway to comment on political, social and environmental matters. We have seen how his social conscience comes to the fore at particular moments, most forcibly in the two years following the *Greendale* tour of spring 2004. He headlined the Clean Air Benefit Concert on 17 September in Vancouver with Randy Bachman and made a series of guest appearances that autumn with Pearl Jam, Dixie Chicks, Bruce Springsteen and REM, performing at six of the 40 Vote for Change concerts held in swing states to rally support for the Democratic candidate, John Kerry, in opposition to George W. Bush's retaliatory foreign policy that had led the nation into what many thought was an illegal war.

Kerry's campaign ultimately faltered, but Young stepped up his protests in the following years, appearing on CNN on 18 April 2006 to accuse President Bush of robbing a '9/11 mentality' from Americans. His album of that year, *Living with War*, was explicitly anti-consumerist. Initially available in a free, downloadable format, and then released on LP and CD with the album title stencilled on a grungy, brown-paper cover, some tracks use heavy guitars to attenuate the critique of consumerism, political mismanagement and failed leadership. The political theme is unrelenting, but musically it is an eclectic album, using a gospel choir and bugle on 'Shock and Awe' to dramatize the cost of war. Young and Springsteen were aghast that there were few musical protests to challenge what liberals saw as a dangerous ideological situation, with Homeland Security threatening civil liberties and military operations lowering the prestige of the United States overseas.[7] This energy fed through to Young's politicized Freedom of Speech tour with CSN that summer, featuring many tracks from *Living with War*.

The use of news-format footage for the *Greendale* and *Living with War* videos shows that Young is willing to harness media outlets, even if he is wary of hype. He exploits the media when it suits him, particularly to promote Pono and in his environmental and nativist projects of 2014, partly inspired by his new activist partner Daryl Hannah and partly by long-term collaborator Willie Nelson. Some interviewers find it hard to delve into complex issues with Young and his social criticism can sometimes be blunt. The video of his 1988 single 'This Note's for You' won an MTV Best Video Award for its slick parody of celebrity product endorsements (despite its initial ban), but his critique of consumerism can descend to a base level, exemplified by the

Vancouver Clean Air Concert poster, 17 September 2004, designed by Bob Masse.

CLEAN AIR CONCERT

2004 NEIL YOUNG
RANDY BACHMAN
BARENAKED LADIES
TAL BACHMAN
COWICHAN CENTRE DUNCAN BC

1994 track 'Piece of Crap', where all capitalist endeavours lead to rubbish, and 'Motor City', where the tensions at the turn of the 1980s between a struggling Detroit car industry and the rise of more efficient Japanese automobile imports is reduced to the one-liner 'who's driving my car now?' Much of his social commentary is emotionally loaded, but he can be more subtle – in his stories of working families on 'This Old House' and 'Ordinary People', for example, or his ecological lament 'Natural Beauty', or the title track of his album *Hawks and Doves* (1980), which hovers between a populist nationalism and a sense, as the Reagan versus Carter presidential race entered its final stage, that Republicans and Democrats need to come together to mend deep partisan rifts.

Most often he is deliberately provocative about social causes because he believes that few in the music industry are willing to take forward the countercultural torch and that music is in danger of being co-opted for ideological ends, such as the unauthorized use of 'Rockin' in the Free World' by business mogul Donald Trump in his announcement in June 2015 that he would be standing as a 2016 u.s. presidential candidate. It was no surprise that Young spoke out against Trump, but he has also periodically distanced himself from his generation, notably from the la folk-rock fraternity in the 1980s, triggered by the ugliest phase of Crosby's freebase habit. He retains a hippie sensibility and sense of wonder, even though he has hardened to the idealism of the 1960s and also to his initial enthusiasm for Barack Obama in the lead-up to the 2008 presidential election. For example, the lead single 'Who's Gonna Stand Up?' from *Storytone* is an act of environmentalist conviction, tinged with despair that there is no natural successor to promote the values that his generation held dear. In October 2014 he even called for President Obama's impeachment for opening the Gulf of Mexico to offshore fracking.[8] Young often takes activism back to first principles, arguing from a romantic perspective that causes begin

L–R: Louis C.K., Neil Young, Jack White and Jimmy Fallon, with the 1940s Voice-O-Graph booth, *The Tonight Show*, 12 May 2014.

with 'you and me'. At root, this song can be seen as a riposte to Dylan's 1980 song 'When You Gonna Wake Up', but with Dylan's born again Christian outlook of that time replaced by a humanist commitment to preserve Mother Earth.

We have seen how Young's mercurial interests travel across a range of styles and topics that move from the highway to the ditch, but the themes of drifting and transformation underpin his many directions. His social causes suggest that he realizes that drifting cannot carry on perpetually or that it sometimes needs an anchor – an attitude that echoes both the defiance and commitment that the Situationists invest in drifting. A belief in movement and change has kept his music fresh and he has continued to explore different American geographies (Mexico, Wyoming, Kansas, Florida, Detroit, New Orleans, Chicago), but with enough continuity to trace arcs through 50 years of writing and performing. Nevertheless, certain images perpetuated in the media tend to fix upon him a signature style that he has at times deliberately shunned, wary never to become the 'park-bench' mutation he rejects in 'Thrasher'. Perhaps inspired by the release in 2009 of the *Neil Young Archives Vol. 1* box set comprising early recordings and solo performances, it is Young the folk balladeer that most frequently resurfaces, rather than the rocker or the experimentalist or the activist.

Jimmy Fallon may have perfected this classic image of Young with his musical skits. In a *Late Night with Jimmy Fallon* show from November 2010 Fallon appeared as the *Harvest*-era Young, playing acoustic guitar and harmonica and gently singing a folky version of Willow Smith's 'Whip My Hair', joined by Bruce Springsteen parodying himself in a *Born to Run* costume; and in July 2014 Fallon's Young was joined by the real Crosby, Stills & Nash to harmonize on Iggy Azalea's 'Fancy', before closing with a coda inspired by 'Suite: Judy Blue Eyes'.[9] Young took Fallon's impressions in good humour when he appeared with fellow traveller Jack White on *The Tonight Show* in May 2014 to promote *A Letter Home*, recording 'Crazy' on the show in White's carefully restored Voice-O-Graph booth and then returning nine months later to perform a duet of 'Old Man' with Fallon.[10] Young's relaxed interviews on these shows combined a genuine commitment to rescue a lost musical technology with enough good humour to realize that Fallon's impersonations are an act of homage to one of music's most enigmatic and enduring performers.

CHRONOLOGY

1945–9

Neil Percival Young is born in Toronto, Ontario, on 12 November 1945 to Scott and Edna ('Rassy') Young. His older brother Bob was born three years earlier. His first home is 335 Brooke Avenue in north Toronto. In August 1949 the family moves to 33 King Street West in Omemee, Ontario, around 80 miles northeast of Toronto.

1950S

In August 1951 Neil contracts polio. For New Year 1952 the family begins a series of extended vacations to New Smyrna Beach, Florida, to help him recuperate from polio.

The family moves to Toronto in 1952, living in three locations: 133 Rose Park Drive, Moore Park; Brock Road, Pickering (east of Toronto); and 49 Old Orchard Grove in north Toronto. While living in Pickering Neil dreams of becoming a chicken farmer.

In summer 1959 Scott and Rassy Young separate (they divorce in 1961) and in August Rassy and Neil move to Winnipeg, Manitoba. Initially they live at 250 Hugo Street, Corydon Avenue, south of downtown, and Neil enrols at Earl Grey Junior High School close by.

1960–64

Young plays his first gig with The Jades at Earl Grey Community Club on 6 January 1961. He plays in three other bands in 1961–2: The Esquires, The Stardusters and The Classics.

Between 1961 and 1964 he is a pupil at Kelvin High School in River Heights. Summer 1962 sees Neil and his mother move to a detached house nearer the school on 1123 Grosvenor Avenue, Crescentwood, but his grades suffer as his interest in playing music grows.

His first serious band The Squires play their first gig on 1 February 1963. They record their only single, 'The Sultan' / 'Aurora', in July, which is released by V Records in November.

Young buys a 1948 Buick Roadmaster, 'Mort', in September 1964 and The Squires play their first show outside Manitoba at the Fourth Dimension Club, Fort William, Ontario, on 1 February 1964. In October the band begins their run at The Flamingo Club, Fort William.

1965

On 18 April 1965 Young meets Stephen Stills and his band The Company at the Fourth Dimension. That summer Mort, The Squires' makeshift tour bus, breaks down near Blind River, Ontario, and Young moves the band to Toronto, where his father lives. The Squires rename themselves Four to Go but find no opportunities to play in Yorkville. As a soloist Young picks up a few gigs at the New Gate of Cleve and the Riverboat Coffee House.

1966

In January 1966 Young joins The Mynah Birds, but the band breaks up in February while they are recording their debut album in Detroit, when the u.s. lead singer Ricky James Matthews is caught avoiding the draft. This hastens Young's decision to drive to Los Angeles in search of Stills, following an unsuccessful trip to find him in New York City the previous October.

On 22 March Young and four companions leave Toronto in 'Mort II', a 1953 Pontiac hearse, to drive the 3,300 miles to Los Angeles. After an enforced stop in Albuquerque, where Young experiences the first signs of epilepsy, Young, Bruce Palmer and another of the original companions arrive at their destination on 1 April.

A week later Neil Young and Bruce Palmer meet Stephen Stills and Richie Furay by chance on Sunset Strip. Their new band, Buffalo Springfield, plays its first show at The Troubadour on 11 April and in May they start playing regularly at the Whisky a Go Go. The band's eponymous debut album is released in December.

Following a brief stint living in a Commodore Gardens apartment on Orchid Avenue, Hollywood, in the summer Young moves to 8451 Utica Drive, Laurel Canyon.

1967

Buffalo Springfield's most popular single, 'For What it's Worth', is released on 28 January. The debut album is rereleased in April with this as the opening track and their second album, *Buffalo Springfield Again*, follows in November.

The band play their first show outside California at the Civic Auditorium, Albuquerque, on 8 February. They tour extensively this year, including a performance at the Monterey Pop Festival on 18 June, temporarily without Young.

1968

Buffalo Springfield tour the South supporting the Beach Boys in April 1968. The band play their final concert at Long Beach Sports Arena on 5 May and their third and final album, *Last Time Around*, is released in July. In August Young moves to 611 Skyline Trail, Topanga Canyon.

As a solo artist Young supports Joni Mitchell in October at The Bitter End, New York City. He plays three nights at Canterbury House, Ann Arbor, Michigan, on 8–10 November, and a selection from these concerts is released as *Sugar Mountain: Live at Canterbury House* in 2008. His debut solo album, *Neil Young*, is released on Reprise Records in November 1968. He marries Susan Acevedo on 1 December.

1969

The only single from *Neil Young*, 'The Loner', appears on 21 February but fails to chart. The album is remixed and reissued in the summer because Young dislikes the original mix.

The Buffalo Springfield compilation album *Retrospective* is released in February and Young's second album, *Everybody Knows This Is Nowhere*, with Crazy Horse (formerly The Rockets), appears in May.

Young joins Crosby, Stills & Nash in late summer to form CSNY. Their first gig as a four-piece is at The Auditorium, Chicago, on 16 August. They also play the Woodstock Music and Art Fair in the early hours of 18 August, the Big Sur Folk Festival on 13–14 September, and the Altamont Free Festival on 6 December.

1970

Crosby, Stills, Nash & Young's debut album, *Déjà Vu*, is released in March. Young writes 'Ohio' in response to the shooting of four students by the National Guard at Kent State University on 4 May; csny release it as a single ('Ohio' / 'Find the Cost of Freedom') in June.

Young's third solo album, *After the Gold Rush*, appears in June, taking its title and some of its themes from Dean Stockwell's unrealized film project of that name.

Young plays shows with Crazy Horse in the spring, including four gigs at the Fillmore East, Boston, on 6–7 March (released in 2006 as *Live at the Fillmore East*). Young joins csny for a u.s. tour in June, and ends the year with a number of solo concerts.

In the summer Young purchases 140 acres of land at the end of Bear Gulch Road, La Honda, in San Mateo County, California. He moves there in September following his divorce from Susan Acevedo. He renames the estate Broken Arrow Ranch. Young starts dating the actress Carrie Snodgress in winter 1970.

1971

Young performs twice at Massey Hall, Toronto, on 19 January; songs from these shows are released in 2007 as *Live at Massey Hall 1971*. He appears on the *Johnny Cash TV Show* on 17 February (alongside James Taylor and Linda Ronstadt) and records an acoustic session in the uk for the bbc on 23 February.

He spends a number of months working at the Quadrafonic Sound Studios, Nashville, with The Stray Gators on a collection of songs for *Harvest*. Nash and Crosby supply backing vocals for other *Harvest* tracks recorded in California, and csny's double live album *Four Way Street* is released in April, from concerts played the previous June and July.

1972

Young's fourth album, *Harvest*, is released in February and his first film, *Journey through the Past* (and a double soundtrack album), appears in November, comprising concert footage from the previous year. He plays only four concerts in 1972. His son Zeke Young is born on 8 September. Crazy Horse singer and guitarist Danny Whitten overdoses on heroin on 18 November and dies.

1973

Young performs on 94 occasions in 1973. The first third of the year is taken up with the *Time Fades Away* tour (with The Stray Gators), the album of which is released in October. The final third of the year is filled with the Tonight's the

Night Club Tour of the u.s., Canada and England with a new band, the Santa Monica Flyers, including Nils Lofgren. The subject of the song 'Tonight's the Night' is the death of their roadie Bruce Berry from a heroin and cocaine overdose on 7 June. The *Tonight's the Night* album is recorded in August, but not released until 1975.

In late May to early June Young is joined by Crosby, Stills and Nash on Maui in Hawaii for a working holiday. On returning to California they twice try to record an album, to be called *Human Highway*, but never complete the project.

1974

Young buys an apartment on Sea Level Drive, Malibu, to gain inspiration for his next studio album, *On the Beach*. It is recorded early in the year at Broken Arrow, Redwood City, California, and Sunset Sound Recorders, Hollywood, and is released in July.

csny play a high-profile tour in the u.s. and Canada between July and September, finishing at Wembley Stadium, London, on 14 September. A compilation album, *So Far*, appears in August that year and a selection from the shows is finally released in 2014 as *csny 1974*. Young visits Amsterdam briefly at the end of the tour and writes the still unreleased 'Frozen Man', reflecting on his difficulties with Carrie Snodgress.

Lynyrd Skynyrd release 'Sweet Home Alabama' as a single and on their *Second Helping* album, partly in response to Young's critical view of the region on 'Southern Man' and 'Alabama'.

1975

Young releases two studio albums in 1975: *Tonight's the Night* in June and *Zuma*, with Crazy Horse, in November. He also records tracks for another album, *Homegrown*, in November and December, a project which remains unreleased at the time of writing.

Snodgress moves out of Broken Arrow Ranch early in 1975. Unsurprisingly, Young does not perform much this year. He begins the *Zuma* tour with Crazy Horse in December, which extends into a tour of Japan and Europe in early 1976.

1976

In the late spring Young tours with Stephen Stills to promote their collaborative album *Long May You Run*. Young pulls out of the tour after nineteen shows, probably because of a sore throat that makes singing painful.

In October he goes on a short coastal bar tour of Northern California with Crazy Horse before embarking on a more extensive u.s. tour. On 25 November he performs at Winterland, San Francisco, as one of The Band's guests. The concert is released as *The Last Waltz*.

1977

This is an important year for Young, with the triple-album retrospective *Decade* appearing in October. Early in the year he completes the unreleased *Chrome Dreams* and then produces *American Stars 'n Bars* in June, including some material from the *Homegrown* and *Chrome Dreams* sessions. Most of his 1977 shows take place in Santa Cruz with The Ducks.

1978

Young releases the folky *Comes a Time* in October, including tracks recorded between 1975 and 1977. Young plays at The Boarding House, San Francisco, in May and then embarks on the *Rust Never Sleeps* tour with Crazy Horse in September and October. The *Rust Never Sleeps* film is recorded at the Cow Palace on 22 October.

He starts recording his co-directed film project *Human Highway* in San Francisco and New Mexico, including a performance of 'Hey Hey, My My (Into the Black)' with new wave band Devo. The film is put on hold due to high costs and is finally completed in 1982.

Young starts a serious relationship with Pegi Morton, and she has a cameo in *Human Highway*. They marry on 2 August and their son Ben Young is born on 28 November.

1979

Rust Never Sleeps and *Live Rust*, released in June and November respectively, capture the energy of the previous autumn's Crazy Horse tour. *Rust Never Sleeps* includes songs originally planned for *Chrome Dreams*. Young does not perform at all in 1979 – his first year as a professional musician without performing. This is partly because Ben Young is diagnosed with cerebral palsy and requires extensive supervision.

1980–84

Young's tenth studio album, *Hawks and Doves*, is released in November 1980, drawn from sessions that go back to 1974. He follows this with *Re-ac-tor* in October 1981, his fifth collaboration with Crazy Horse. At the end of 1982 he releases his first album on the Geffen label, the electronic *Trans*, on which he reflects on his son Ben's communication difficulties.

He performs only one show in each of 1980 and 1981, but then springs back to life as a performer with the Trans band on a U.S. tour in summer 1982 and a European leg in the autumn, including a number of concerts in Germany, as captured on *Neil Young in Berlin*. He plays 75 North American concerts in 1983 on the solo *Trans* tour.

Human Highway makes its cinematic debut in Los Angeles in June 1983. Arguably his worst-ever album, the 25-minute *Everybody's Rockin'*, with the rockabilly band The Shocking Pinks, is released in August 1983, much to the displeasure of Dave Geffen, who believes that Young was being deliberately obstreperous.

1984 begins with a number of concerts with Crazy Horse, but is then dominated by a major tour with the old-time country band International Harvesters. The tour continues through 1985, including a leg in Australia and New Zealand. Songs from this 1984–5 International Harvesters tour appear on *A Treasure*, released in 2011. Neil and Pegi Young's daughter Amber Jean is born on 15 May 1984.

1985–9

The second half of the 1980s begins with a struggle to leave Geffen Records. For contractual reasons Young's August 1985 release *Old Ways* is not the album he had originally planned. He follows *Old Ways* with *Landing on Water* and *Life* in 1986 and 1987. His return to critical acclaim comes via *This Note's for You* in April 1988 and *Freedom* in October 1989. In between these projects he releases a CSNY reunion album, *American Dream*, and is acclaimed by alternative bands on *The Bridge: A Tribute to Neil Young*.

The International Harvesters Tour of 1984–5 is followed by their appearance at Live Aid on 13 July 1985 (plus two songs by CSNY) and the first Farm Aid concert on 22 September in Champaign, Illinois. The first Bridge School Benefit concert follows on 13 October 1986, for which CSNY play a twelve-song set. This is sandwiched between a series of Crazy Horse concerts, dubbed Live in a Rusted Out Garage, followed by 72 North American and European concerts in 1987, with both Crazy Horse and the Blue Notes, the latter of which continue through to September 1988.

In 1989 Young plays 64 concerts, many of them in Australia, Japan and Europe, spanning his back catalogue and new songs from *Freedom*.

1990–94

The 1990s begin with the death of Young's mother Rassy and a musical return to critical and popular acclaim. This starts with two releases with Crazy Horse, the studio album *Ragged Glory* in September 1990 and the *Arc/Weld* live experimental project, released in October 1991, capturing the essence of the North American shows in the early part of the year, as the Gulf War is drawing to a close.

This is followed by a return to the relaxed country feel of the early 1970s with the release of *Harvest Moon* in October 1992, the soundtrack for Jim Jarmusch's psychedelic Western *Dead Man*, and an impressive performance on MTV *Unplugged* on 7 February 1993, which is released on record that June. Less impressive is his compilation release *Lucky Thirteen*, comprised of tracks written while on the Geffen label between 1982 and 1988. His homage to the death of Nirvana singer Kurt Cobain gives him the title of his August 1994 release with Crazy Horse, *Sleeps with Angels*.

Live performances are dominated by the four-month Smell the Horse tour of early 1991, an extensive solo tour of 1992 (with a focus on *Harvest Moon* tracks, released as *Dreamin' Man Live '92* in 2009) and a transatlantic tour with Booker T. & the MG's in 1993. This follows the band's appearance at the Bob Dylan 30th Anniversary Concert on 16 October 1992 at Madison Square Gardens.

1995–9

Young is inducted into the Rock and Roll Hall of Fame in 1995, introduced by Eddie Vedder, the lead singer of the Seattle grunge band Pearl Jam. The choice of Vedder reflects Young and Pearl Jam's collaboration on *Mirror Ball* and a tour of the U.S., Europe and Israel. In November 1995 David Briggs, Young's producer since his debut album of 1968, dies; three months later the soundtrack of Jim Jarmusch's *Dead Man* is released.

Mirror Ball is followed by another Crazy Horse project, *Broken Arrow*, in July 1996, the vinyl version of which also includes 'Interstate', previously recorded as an outtake from *Ragged Glory*.

There is only a single live album in this period: the June 1997 release of *Year of the Horse*, on the back of Jim Jarmusch's documentary of that name. The film draws on concert and interview footage of the extensive *Broken Arrow* tour of the U.S., Canada and Europe of 1996. Young and Crazy Horse play a series of HORDE (Horizons of Rock Developing Everywhere) Festival appearances in the second half of 1997. The millennium closes with a three-leg solo tour, from March to June 1999, and another CSNY album, the underwhelming *Looking Forward*.

2000–2004

The gentle *Silver & Gold* of April 2000, recorded between 1997 and 1999 in Woodside, California, is followed in April 2002 by Young's 25th studio album, *Are You Passionate?*, with Booker T. & the MG's (including his response to 9/11 in the single 'Let's Roll' and the searching title track) and the concept album *Greendale* with Crazy Horse in August 2003. The self-directed film *Greendale* is released a year later. Young works on *Greendale* while resident on Green Street, San Francisco, near his daughter Amber's school.

2003 is a year in which Young rediscovers his activist voice, which leads to him championing environmentalist causes and joining the Vote for Change concert series in autumn 2004.

The new millennium begins with two tours: the CSNY 2K tour and the Music in Head tour, with friends and relatives, released as *Road Rock Vol. 1* in November 2000. He steps up his touring with a series of South American and European concerts alongside Crazy Horse the following year and goes back on the road again as CSNY in early 2002.

The European Solo and Acoustic tour and the *Greendale* tour with Crazy Horse make 2003 one of his busiest performing years, including dates in Japan and Australia, before a few final dates in the U.S. in early 2004. That year also sees the release of a *Greatest Hits* album.

2005–9

The year 2005 witnesses the death of Young's father Scott Young after years of fighting Alzheimer's disease, an experience that features that year on *Prairie Wind*, along with a reflection on Young's own brain aneurysm in March for which he has to undergo neurological surgery. Three more studio albums are released in this period: a scathing attack on George W. Bush's foreign policy on 2006's *Living with War* (plus a stripped-down version, *Living with War: In the*

Beginning); *Chrome Dreams II* in October 2007 (a teasing sequel to the unreleased *Chrome Dreams*); and his 30th studio album, *Fork in the Road*, in April 2009. CSNY's politicized Freedom of Speech tour of 2006 is the highest-profile concert series of this period and includes a number of tracks from *Living with War*.

Young promotes *Chrome Dreams II* on his North American and European concerts of 2007–8 and plays extensively with a more mixed set list in 2009. On 26 June 2009 Young headlines the Glastonbury Festival in Somerset and the following day performs at the Hard Rock Calling Festival in Hyde Park, London, 40 years to the month after the famous Rolling Stones concert there.

February 2006 sees the first of a trilogy of concert films from Jonathan Demme with the cinematic release of *Neil Young: Heart of Gold*, documenting his concerts at the Ryman Auditorium on 18 and 19 August 2005, including a number of tracks from *Prairie Wind*. The second of the trilogy, *Neil Young Trunk Show*, contains rare live tracks and is deliberately more intimate. It opens at the Toronto Film Festival in 2009 but as of the time of writing has been unreleased on DVD. The third film in the sequence, *Neil Young Journeys* from 2011, takes Young back on a road trip to Omemee, interspersed with songs from *Le Noise* and his back catalogue.

The first volume of the *Neil Young Archives* project is released in June 2009. This eight-disc set spans the period 1963 to 1972 and follows soon after the appearance of live recordings from this period in the Performance Series. The 1972 film *Journey through the Past* is also made available for the first time on the ten-disc DVD/Blu-ray version of *Archives Vol. I*.

2010–14

In September 2010 Young releases the first solo electric album *Le Noise*, produced by fellow Canadian Daniel Lanois. The second track, 'Walk with Me', reflects on the death in July of long-time collaborator Ben Keith, who had worked consistently with Young since 1971.

This period proves to be a very active one for Young, with two volumes of memoirs released: *Waging Heavy Peace* in 2012 and *Special Deluxe* in 2014. These two years also see the release of four album projects: in 2012 the double studio album *Psychedelic Pill* and a record of idiosyncratic folk standards, *Americana*, both with Crazy Horse; a solo album of covers, *A Letter Home*, appears in April 2014, recorded in Jack White's 1940s Voice-O-Graph booth; and the autobiographical *Storytone* is released that November. For *Storytone* Young makes use of a full orchestra for all the tracks on the standard album and adds an acoustic set of the same songs on the deluxe version.

Young performs solo on his three-leg Twisted Road tour of 2010–11, before playing seven shows with a reunited Buffalo Springfield in June 2011. These two years see the 25th anniversaries of Farm Aid and the Bridge School Benefit concerts, in October 2010 and November 2011 respectively. In 2011 Young begins work on his portable digital music device, Pono.

A series of Crazy Horse concerts from 2012 ends with a benefit event for Hurricane Sandy victims in Atlantic City, New Jersey, on 6 December, before kicking back into the extensive Alchemy Tour of 2013 through North America, Europe and Australia. Another Performance Series recording, *Live at the Cellar Door*, drawn from six 1970 solo concerts, appears in December 2013.

The year 2014 is a very busy one for Young. He tours as a solo artist and with Crazy Horse and works towards the release of Pono. Pono is formally announced at the sxsw Festival in March and then launched at the Dreamforce conference in mid-October. He also plays four concerts in Toronto, Winnipeg, Regina, Saskatchewan and Calgary on the Honour the Treaties tour in protest against the polluting effects of the oil fields near Fort McMurray, Alberta.

In 2014 the media, fuelled by the fact that he has filed for divorce from Pegi Young, reports that Young has started dating Daryl Hannah.

2015

In June 2015 Young releases a third version of *Storytone* on vinyl, *Mixed Pages of Storytone*, which interweaves orchestral and solo songs, and a new studio album, *The Monsanto Years*, featuring Willie Nelson's sons, Lukas and Micah, as showcased in the summer Rebel Content Tour with Lukas Nelson's band Promise of the Real.

Pono finally goes on sale in January and, with a re-cut version of *Human Highway* in circulation, it is likely that *Neil Young Archives Vol. 2* will be soon released.

In November Young celebrates his 70th birthday, 50 years since he struggled to find gigs in the coffee houses and bars of Toronto.

REFERENCES

INTRODUCTION: TWISTED ROAD

1 Cameron Crowe, 'So Hard to Make Arrangements for Yourself', *Rolling Stone* (13 August 1975), in Rolling Stone, *Neil Young: The Rolling Stone Files*, introduction by Holly George-Warren (New York, 1994), p. 124. For Young's thoughts on his control freakery see his uncut interview with Tim Roth, accompanying a VH1 *Centerstage* performance at WTTW studios, Chicago, 17 November 1992, released as the bootleg DVD *Neil Young: VH1 Centerstage* in 1993.

2 Jeremy Deller, *Time Out* interview (2012), www.timeout.com.

3 Interview with Elliot Roberts, in Jimmy McDonough, *Shakey: Neil Young's Biography* (London, 2002), p. 241.

4 For the death rumour linked to his dishevelled state on the Tonight's the Night Club Tour of autumn 1973 see Scott Young, *Neil and Me* (Toronto, [1984] 2009), pp. 192–3.

5 McDonough, *Shakey*, p. 48.

6 William Echard, *Neil Young and the Poetics of Energy* (Bloomington, IN, 2005).

7 Scott Young, *Neil and Me*, p. 216.

8 Neil Young, *Special Deluxe: A Memoir of Life and Cars* (New York, 2014), p. 43.

9 For discussion of Young and Orbison see Sharry Wilson, *Young Neil: The Sugar Mountain Years* (Toronto, 2014), pp. 226–7; and Nick Kent, 'The Young will Run and Run', *Vox* (November 1990), available at www.rocksbackpages.com (accessed January 2015).

10 Greil Marcus, *Like a Rolling Stone: Bob Dylan at the Crossroads* (London, 2006), p. 10.

11 For a parallel discussion of Dylan's *Street Legal* and Young's *Comes a Time* and their contrasting New York City concerts see Jay Cocks, 'Dylan and Young on the Road', *Time* (6 November 1978), p. 89. See also John Rockwell, 'Neil Young – As Good as Bob Dylan?', *New York Times* (19 June 1977), and Daniel Durchholz and Gary Graff, *Neil Young: Long May You Run – The Illustrated History* (Minneapolis, MN, 2010), pp. 18–19.

12 For discussion of the evolution of 'I Wonder' see John Einarson, *Neil Young: Don't Be Denied – The Canadian Years* (Ketchum, IN, [1993] 2012), pp. 116, 142–3.

13 Young admitted he was surprised how similar 'Ambulance Blues' was to 'Needle of Death': Jan Osbrecht, 'In the Eye of the Hurricane', *Guitar Player* (March 1992), p. 54.

14 Sean Wilentz, *Bob Dylan in America* (London, 2010), p. 8.

15 Ibid., p. 9.

16 See Robert A. Wright, '"Dream, Comfort, Memory, Despair": Canadian Popular Musicians and the Dilemma of Nationalism, 1968–1972', in *Canadian Music: Issues of Hegemony and Identity*, ed. Beverley Diamond and Robert Witmer (Toronto, 1994), p. 291. Michael Heatley, *Neil Young: In His Own Words* (London, 1997), p. 9.

17 Guy Debord, *Society of the Spectacle*, trans. Fredy Perlman (London, [1967] 1977), thesis 59.

18 Ibid., thesis 170.

19 For Jenice Heo's 2010 Neil Young Series see www.jeniceheo.com/neil-young-series. The website also carries a 2012 article by Andy Brumer, 'We are Only what we Feel'.

20 Jenice Heo, *Where is the Highway Tonight?*, from Neil Young Series.

21 Kent, 'The Young will Run and Run'.

22 This view of space corresponds with that broadly shared by a group of contemporary American travel writers, as discussed in Wendy Harding's *The Myth of Emptiness and the New American Literature of Place* (Iowa City, IA, 2014).

23 Linda Ronstadt interviewed by Joe Pascal at the Hudson Union Society, September 2013.

24 McDonough, *Shakey*, p. 215.

25 Young, *Special Deluxe*, p. 106.

26 Debord, *Society of the Spectacle*, thesis 158.

27 Ibid., thesis 187.

28 Cited in David Zimmer, *4 Way Street: The Crosby, Stills, Nash & Young Reader* (New York, 2004), p. 26.

29 Young's LincVolt website outlines his ideas for a future of clean automobiles; see www.lincvolt.com.

1 MANITOBA AND ONTARIO

1　The Squires was actually Young's fifth band as a teenager, but the first to break out of the Winnipeg school circuit.

2　For the rise of the music scene in Yorkville see Stuart Henderson, *Making the Scene: Yorkville and Hip Toronto in the 1960s* (Toronto, 2011).

3　John Einarson, *Neil Young: Don't Be Denied – The Canadian Years* (Ketchum, IN, [1993] 2012), p. 231.

4　Mike Marqusee, *Wicked Messenger: Bob Dylan and the 1960s* (New York, [2003] 2005), p. 204.　.

5　Stephen Stills, quoted in Dave Zimmer, *Crosby, Stills & Nash* (New York, [1984] 2008), p. 30.

6　For a discussion of the first encounter between Young and Stills see Johnny Rogan, *Neil Young: Zero to Sixty – A Critical Biography* (London, 2000), pp. 37–9.

7　See Sharry Wilson, *Young Neil: The Sugar Mountain Years* (Toronto, 2014), pp. 43, 54.

8　Young wrote both tracks. The band gave his 'Image in Blue' instrumental the alternative title 'Aurora' during the recording session of 23 July 1963. See Wilson, *Young Neil*, pp. 265–71, and Neil Young, *Special Deluxe: A Memoir of Life and Cars* (New York, 2014), pp. 63–4.

9　Marqusee, *Wicked Messenger*, p. 205.

10　Quoted in Michael Heatley, *Neil Young: In His Own Words* (London, 1994), p. 8.

11　Ernest Hemingway, *A Moveable Feast* (London, [1964] 2011), p. 19.

12　Rickie Lee Jones, cited in Jimmy McDonough, *Shakey: Neil Young's Biography* (New York, 2002), p. 15.

13　Neil Young, *Waging Heavy Peace* (London, 2012), pp. 27–8.

14　See Young's foreword to William DeKay, *Down Home: A Journey into Rural Canada* (Toronto, 1997), p. 11.

15　Ed Ward, '"Sugar Mountain" Single Review' (3 September 1970), in Rolling Stone, *Neil Young: The Rolling Stone Files*, introduction by Holly George-Warren (New York, 1994), p. 66. For a comparison of 'Sugar Mountain' and the folk standard 'Big Rock Candy Mountain' see Jason Schneider, *Whispering Pines: The Northern Roots of American Music* (Toronto, 2009), p. 243.

16　McDonough, *Shakey*, p. 124.

17　Cited in John Einarson and Richie Furay, *Buffalo Springfield: For What it's Worth* (London, 1997), p. 52. For an extended discussion of Ross 'Clancy' Smith see Wilson, *Young Neil*, pp. 197–202.

18　See also Maynard Collins, *Lightfoot: If You could Read His Mind* (Toronto, 1988), p. 143.

19　See Schneider, *Whispering Pines*, p. 121.

20 Robert A. Wright, '"Dream, Comfort, Memory, Despair": Canadian Popular Musicians and the Dilemma of Nationalism, 1968–1972', in *Canadian Music: Issues of Hegemony and Identity*, ed. Beverley Diamond and Robert Witmer (Toronto, 1994), p. 284.

21 McDonough, *Shakey*, p. 325. George McKay views the song through the filter of polio, especially as Young and Joni Mitchell (both of them childhood polio sufferers) duet on the song for The Band's 1976 *The Last Waltz* concert: McKay, *Shakin' All Over: Popular Music and Disability* (Ann Arbor, MI, 2013), p. 33.

22 Journalist Richie Yorke claimed that the applause at Young's 1971 Massey Hall concerts surpassed any other he had heard there: quoted in Schneider, *Whispering Pines*, p. 261.

23 Bud Scoppa, review of *Time Fades Away* (3 January 1974), in *Neil Young: The Rolling Stone Files*, p. 96. For school bullying see Wilson, *Young Neil*, p. 81.

24 Young, *Special Deluxe*, p. 68. McDonough, *Shakey*, p. 97. For the status of 'Four Strong Winds' within Canadian cultural history see John Einarson, *Four Strong Winds* (Toronto, 2011), pp. 6–8, 104–6; and Schneider, *Whispering Pines*, pp. 105–6.

25 For an exploration of Alberta folk songs see T. B. Rogers, 'Is there an Alberta Folk Music?', *Canadian Folk Music Journal*, VI (1978), pp. 23–9; and Cheryl J. Hendrickson, 'English Language Folk Music in Alberta', *Canadian Folk Music Journal*, X (1982), pp. 34–9.

26 Carol Shields, *The Stone Diaries* (Toronto, 1993), p. 27. Young's voice has been described as 'like the wind on the Prairies': Douglas Fetherling, *Some Day Soon: Essays on Canadian Songwriters* (Dallas, TX, 1991), p. 136.

27 See Young, *Special Deluxe*, p. 29.

28 David Fricke, 'Neil Young Q&A', *Rolling Stone* (22 May 2014), p. 30; and Young, *Special Deluxe*, pp. 27–8.

29 For a reflection on the effects of the Fort McMurray oil sands on the 'Canadian jewel' Alberta, see Young, *Special Deluxe*, pp. 355–9, 375–6. The oil sands are depicted on the cover of the 12-inch vinyl release of 'Who's Gonna Stand Up?'

30 Written in 1961, 'I was Young When I Left Home' was Dylan's take on the traditional 'Nine Hundred Miles'. Recorded at the same time as the group of songs that appeared on Dylan's first album, the track was not released until 2005 on *The Bootleg Series Volume 7: No Direction Home: The Soundtrack*.

2 LOS ANGELES

1 Neil Young, *Waging Heavy Peace* (New York, 2012), p. 128.

2 Ibid., pp. 127–8.

3   See, for example, Richie Unterberger, *Turn! Turn! Turn! The '60s Folk-rock Revolution* (San Francisco, CA, 2002), p. 221.

4   The *Toronto Star* published an evocative description of Young's Topanga Canyon home on 1 February 1969, quoted in Scott Young, *Neil and Me* (Toronto, [1984] 2009), pp. 95–6.

5   Kevin Starr, *Golden Dreams: California in an Age of Abundance, 1950–1963* (Oxford, 2009), p. 175.

6   Michael Walker, *Laurel Canyon* (New York, 2006), p. 16.

7   Fred Goodman, *The Mansion on the Hill* (New York, 1998), p. 68.

8   Domenic Priore, *Riot on Sunset Strip: Rock 'n' Roll's Last Stand in Hollywood* (London, 2007), pp. 242–57. Young mentions Pandora's Box in Neil Young, *Special Deluxe: A Memoir of Life and Cars* (New York, 2014), p. 104.

9   Linda Ronstadt quoted in John Einarson, *Desperados: The Roots of Country Rock* (New York, 2001), p. 11.

10 Jimmy McDonough, *Shakey: Neil Young's Biography* (New York, 2002), p. 169.

11 Young, *Waging Heavy Peace*, p. 131. Young gave a revealing interview on CBC radio on 11 February 1969 about the folding of Buffalo Springfield and the launch of his solo album. Barney Hoskyns draws a rather ugly portrait of Stills in *Hotel California: Singer-songwriters and Cocaine Cowboys in the LA Canyons, 1967–1976* (London, 2006), p. 45.

12 See John Einarson and Richie Furay, *For What it's Worth: The Story of Buffalo Springfield* (Lanham, MD, 1997), pp. 141–2.

13 George McKay, *Shakin' All Over: Popular Music and Disability* (Ann Arbor, MI, 2013), pp. 108–10.

14 Einarson and Furay, *For What it's Worth*, pp. 150, 156.

15 Cécile Whiting, *Pop LA: Art and the City in the 1960s* (Berkeley, CA, 2008), p. 205.

16 Ken Lynch, *The Image of the City* (Cambridge, MA, 1960), p. 33.

17 Mike Davis, *City of Quartz: Excavating the Future in Los Angeles* (London, 1990); and Alison Lurie, *The Nowhere City* (New York, 1965).

18 Whiting, *Pop LA*, pp. 205–6.

19 See Reyner Banham, *Los Angeles: The Architecture of Four Ecologies* (Berkeley, CA, [1971] 2009), p. 193.

20 Lynch, *The Image of the City*, p. 34.

21 Bruce Miroff, *Everybody Knows This Is Nowhere* album review, *Rolling Stone* (9 August 1969), in Rolling Stone, *Neil Young: The Rolling Stone Files*, introduction by Holly George-Warren (New York, 1994), p. 32.

22 Charles Manson featured on the 25 June 1970 cover of *Rolling Stone*, an issue which also included a review of Young's protest song 'Ohio'. Manson wrote a talk song entitled 'Sick City' (with the words 'Walking all alone / Not

going anywhere') around the time that Young composed the first draft of 'LA'. 'Sick City' was not released until March 1970 on *Lie: The Love and Terror Cult*, following Manson's arrest for the Laurel Canyon murders.

23 CBC interview, 11 February 1969.

24 See McDonough, *Shakey*, pp. 331–2.

25 Cameron Crowe, 'So Hard to Make Arrangements for Yourself', *Neil Young: The Rolling Stone Files*, p. 129.

26 Young, *Waging Heavy Peace*, pp. 182–3.

27 This phrase is adapted from 'the dark edge of hippie life', a line on the cover of the 19 December 1969 issue of *Life*, featuring Manson and the headline 'The Love and Terror Cult'.

28 For the argument that cocaine was one of the chief factors in the unravelling of the Laurel Canyon scene see Hoskyns, *Hotel California*, pp. 226–31.

3 THE DEEP SOUTH

1 Neil Young, *Waging Heavy Peace* (New York, 2012), p. 458.

2 CBC interview, 11 February 1969. In this interview Young discusses the closing track on his debut solo album, 'The Last Trip to Tulsa', and mentions the Deep South and West Coast.

3 Lewis M. Killian, *White Southerners* (New York, 1970), p. xi.

4 For a description of the Oakland incident see Johnny Rogan, *Neil Young: Zero to Sixty – A Critical Biography* (London, 2000), p. 292.

5 See Dorian Lynskey, 'Neil Young's Ohio – The Greatest Protest Record', *The Guardian* (6 May 2010); and Dorian Lynskey, *33 Revolutions Per Minute: A History of Protest Songs* (London, 2010), pp. 216–17.

6 See Jimmy McDonough, *Shakey: Neil Young's Biography* (New York, 2002), p. 346. Forty years later Young was shown playing an impassioned solo version of 'Ohio' in the documentary film *Neil Young Journeys*.

7 Howard Stern Show, 14 October 2014, howardstern.com (accessed January 2015). The composition of the song has been heavily mythologized: Crosby misremembers that Young's inspiration was John Filo's famous image of fourteen-year-old Mary Ann Vecchio kneeling over the dead body of Jeffrey Miller and Stills thinks that he was reacting to television footage: see the CNN special report *Witnessed: The Killings at Kent State*, 4 May 2014.

8 The horsemen also appear in silhouette on the soundtrack album and film poster.

9 McDonough, *Shakey*, pp. 337–8.

10 Rogan, *Neil Young: Zero to Sixty*, p. 277.

11 Mark Kemp, *Dixie Lullaby: A Story of Music, Race and New Beginnings in the South* (Athens, GA, 2006), p. 91. For a broader comparison of West Coast responses to the South – including Randy Newman, Warren Zevon and Tom Petty, as well as Young – see George Plasketes, 'Anthems, Antagonists, and Accents: The Beat and Off-Beat of the American South', *Studies in Popular Culture*, XIX/2 (October 1996), pp. 197–215.

12 Cited in Kemp, *Dixie Lullaby*, p. 92. For the uncertain source of Ronnie Van Zant's quotation, reputedly from a 1976 British radio interview, see Kemp's note on pp. 266–7.

13 There is a rumour that Van Zant was buried in his Neil Young T-shirt: see Daniel Durchholz and Gary Graff, *Neil Young: Long May You Run – The Illustrated History* (Minneapolis, MN, 2010), p. 61.

14 Randy McNutt, *Guitar Towns: A Journey to the Crossroads of Rock 'n' Roll* (Bloomington, IN, 2002), p. 126.

15 For the Gregg Allman comment see Alan Paul, *One Way Out: The Inside History of the Allman Brothers Band* (New York, 2014), p. 99. U2 played a fast-tempo version of 'Southern Man' on *The Old Grey Whistle Test* (BBC2) in 1987, adapting the lyrics to make it relevant to the Irish experience.

16 There are interesting connections between the silver fiddle on 'See the Sky about to Rain' and the golden fiddle on the Charlie Daniel's Band's 'The Devil Went down to Georgia', as popularized in the 1980 film *Urban Cowboy*. In this song the devil is a skilled musician who outplays the Southern fiddle player. I am grateful to Robert Jones II for this point.

17 Jerome L. Rodnitzky, 'The Decline of Contemporary Protest Music', *Popular Music and Society*, I (Fall 1971), pp. 44, 49–50.

18 See Martyn Bone, *The Postsouthern Sense of Place in Contemporary Fiction* (Baton Rouge, LA, 2014).

19 For the critical reception of *Harvest* see Rogan, *Neil Young: Zero to Sixty*, p. 272.

20 Dylan had been the first guest on the *Johnny Cash Show* on 7 June 1969.

21 Paul Hemphill, *The Nashville Sound: Bright Lights and Country Music* (New York, 1970), p. 163. For the de-regionalization of Southern music in the 1960s and 1970s see Bill C. Malone and David Stricklin, *Southern Music/American Music* (Lexington, KY, [1979] 2003), p. 109.

22 Young played with the Stray Gators at Bakersfield Civic Auditorium in March 1973, including six songs with Crosby and Nash. For discussion of the Bakersfield sound see Gerald W. Haslam, *Workin' Man Blues: Country Music in California* (Berkeley, CA, 1999) and of the fusion of country and other musical traditions see Peter Doggett, *Are You Ready for the Country? Elvis, Dylan, Parsons and the Roots of Country Rock* (London, 2000). Despite taking his title from

Young's 1972 song, Doggett fails to deal with Young's contribution to country music in much depth.

23 For the interviews of 1989 and 1990 see www.thrasherswheat.org/ptma/reagan.htm, and for discussion see Rogan, *Neil Young: Zero to Sixty*, pp. 502–3, 514–15.

24 Parke Puterbaugh, *Old Ways* album review (24 October 1985), in Rolling Stone, *Neil Young: The Rolling Stone Files*, introduction by Holly George-Warren (New York, 1994), pp. 232–3.

25 Haslam, *Workin' Man Blues*, p. 245.

26 For discussion of the origins of *Old Ways* and the 1984–5 tour see Rogan, *Neil Young: Zero to Sixty*, pp. 476–7, 498–502.

27 Hemphill, *The Nashville Sound*, p. 33.

28 Rogan describes *Everybody's Rockin'* as 'calculated whimsy' and McDonough describes it as 'surreal theater', arguing that Elvis does not always emerge positively in Young's music: Rogan, *Neil Young: Zero to Sixty*, p. 479, and McDonough, *Shakey*, p. 578.

29 Young wore an Elvis T-shirt under his jacket for his 1988 Vox Pop Raw & Uncooked Interview focusing on *This Note's for You*, available on YouTube, accessed 2 June 2015.

30 Johnny Rogan assumes that 'Hank' refers to Hank Marvin of The Shadows, an early influence on The Squires, but it could even be the pioneering country singer Hank Snow, who left Nova Scotia for Nashville in 1945.

31 Young has compared the impact of Dylan's voice to that of Woody Guthrie and Hank Williams: McDonough, *Shakey*, p. 143.

32 'Neil Young Interview on Guitars', *Guitare & Claviers*, 149 (April 1992). See also 'His Old Guitars', *Guitar World Acoustic* (December 2005), p. 30.

4 NORTHERN CALIFORNIA

1 Neil Young, *Special Deluxe: A Memoir of Life and Cars* (New York, 2014), pp. 132–3. Young's drive from Topanga Canyon up to La Honda was actually in a yellow and black 1951 Jeepster convertible: ibid., pp. 130, 133–4.

2 Young uses this phrase in his introduction to 'Old Man' in the *Heart of Gold* documentary (2006).

3 This view corresponds with Barney Hoskyn's reading of 'Wooden Ships' as a song of 'elitist escapism', although he overlooks the fact that the sailors in the song are from opposite sides of the war: Barney Hoskyns, *Hotel California: Singer-songwriters and Cocaine Cowboys in the LA Canyons, 1967–1976* (Hoboken, NJ, 2007), p. 102.

4   For Crosby's drug meltdown in the 1980s see David Crosby and Carl Gottlieb, *Long Time Gone: The Autobiography of David Crosby* (New York, 1988), pp. 339–439.

5   Quoted in Jimmy McDonough, *Shakey: Neil Young's Biography* (New York, 2002), p. 368.

6   Young recalls having 'no interest in being part' of the Monterey Festival: Young, *Special Deluxe*, p. 109.

7   Joel Selvin, *Monterey Pop: June 16–18, 1967* (San Francisco, CA, 1992), p. 5; Hoskyns, *Hotel California*, p. 15.

8   Nadya Zimmerman, *Counterculture Kaleidoscope: Musical and Cultural Perspectives on Late Sixties San Francisco* (Ann Arbor, MI, [2008] 2013), pp. 101–3.

9   Hank Harrison, *The Dead Book: A Social History of the Haight-Ashbury Experience* (San Francisco, CA, 1973), p. 162.

10 R. Jeffrey Lustig, 'The War at Home: California's Struggle to Stop the Vietnam War', in *What's Going On? California and the Vietnam Era*, ed. Marcia A. Eymann and Charles Wollenberg (Berkeley, CA, 2004), p. 71.

11 Harrison, *The Dead Book*, p. 26.

12 McDonough, *Shakey*, p. 200.

13 Young, *Special Deluxe*, pp. 304–5.

14 For the development of the roots of the San Francisco sound see Craig Morrison, 'Folk Revival Roots Still Evident in 1990s Recordings of San Francisco Psychedelic Veterans', *Journal of American Folklore*, CXIV / 454 (Autumn 2001), pp. 478–88.

15 Zimmerman, *Counterculture Kaleidoscope*, p. 21.

16 Quoted in Michael Lydon, 'The Dead Zone', *Rolling Stone*, 40 (23 August 1969), reprinted in *Rolling Stone: Jerry Garcia*, Special Collector's Edition (August 2014), p. 38. For Garcia's different views of the acid tests see Carol Brightman, *Sweet Chaos: The Grateful Dead's American Adventure* (New York, 1998), pp. 47–8.

17 Ralph J. Gleason, *The Jefferson Airplane and the San Francisco Sound* (New York, 1969), p. 11.

18 Tom Wolfe, *The Electric Kool-Aid Acid Test* (New York, 1968), p. 245. In 1962 The Grateful Dead lyricist Robert Hunter had been involved in the same Stanford University experiments with LSD as Ken Kesey, experiments covertly sponsored by the CIA in the belief that LSD could be an effective 'truth drug' to use in military operations.

19 Ibid., pp. 55–6.

20 Ibid., p. 178.

21 Ibid., p. 54.

22 See 'The Ken Kesey Movie', *Rolling Stone* (7 March 1970), pp. 29–30.

23 Ken Kesey intended to release The Merry Pranksters' home movie of the 1964 transcontinental road trip as 'Intrepid Traveler and His Merry Band of Pranksters Look for a Kool Place'. The footage appeared in parts during Kesey's later years, and was included in a 2011 documentary *Magic Trip*, funded by the Martin Scorsese film foundation. Young's journey from the Californian coast to Washington, DC, in his LincVolt in autumn 2013 could be interpreted as a tamer and more socially conscious restaging of the Merry Pranksters' trip.

24 When he started writing *Greendale* in 2001 the Youngs and their daughter Amber were temporarily living on Green Street in San Francisco: Young, *Special Deluxe*, p. 303.

25 A family tree and a potted biography of the chief characters were published in a showbill of the *Greendale* tour of 2003.

26 This is confirmed by Young's prefatory comments ('don't feel bad if you feel a little out of it with this. No one really knows . . .') in the spin-off graphic novel targeted at teenagers: Josh Dysart, *Neil Young's Greendale* (New York, 2010). The book explores Sun Green's adventurous spirit and environmentalist conscience in greater detail than the album and taps into the legacy of female members of the Green family.

27 On the everyday nature of Jed's transformation into the devil see Sue Sorensen, 'David Byrne and Neil Young as Film Directors', *Studies in Popular Culture*, xxx/1 (Fall 2007), p. 120.

28 For these reviews see David Segal, 'Neil Young's Dysfunctional Family Saga', *Washington Post* (20 August 2003), and Neil Strauss, 'Mapping a Town in Neil Young Land', *New York Times* (18 August 2003).

29 Sorensen, 'David Byrne and Neil Young', pp. 108, 116.

30 This description is by speech pathologist Holly Hamilton, included in *The Bridge School Story* documentary on the 2011 *Bridge School Benefit: 25th Anniversary Edition* DVD. For discussion within the framework of disability, see George McKay, *Shakin' All Over: Popular Music and Disability* (Ann Arbor, MI, 2013), pp. 176–7.

5 DREAM TRAVELLER

1 Jimmy McDonough, *Shakey: Neil Young's Biography* (New York, 2002), p. 489. The *Zuma* imagery was reprised on the travelling dream song 'The Old Homestead' (written in 1975, but unreleased until *Hawks and Doves* in 1980) in the images of 'a prehistoric bird' and 'the naked rider'.

2   For a discussion of myth in progressive rock see Paul Hegarty and Martin
    Halliwell, *Beyond and Before: Progressive Rock since the 1960s* (New York, 2011),
    pp. 85–104.

3   Johnny Rogan, *Neil Young: Zero to Sixty – A Critical Biography* (London, 2000),
    p. 386. The image of fossilization might be prompted by 'Frozen Man', an
    unreleased song written in Amsterdam at the end of CSNY's 1974 tour.

4   McDonough, *Shakey*, p. 491.

5   Johnny Rogan links the figures of the king and queen to the Kennedys and
    Camelot, a theory which would connect the first and third verses via the
    image of the 'black limousine': Rogan, *Neil Young: Zero to Sixty*, pp. 147–8.

6   McDonough, *Shakey*, p. 128.

7   For an impressive interpretation of Dylan's and Hendrix's contrasting
    versions of 'All along the Watchtower' see Albin J. Zak III, 'Bob Dylan and
    Jimi Hendrix: Juxtaposition and Transformation "All along the Watchtower"',
    Journal of the American Musicological Society, LVII/3 (Fall 2004), pp. 599–600.

8   McDonough, *Shakey*, p. 495.

9   Joe Hoyle, 'Fatsound: In Search of Guitar Tone', www.fatsound.wordpress.com,
    26 May 2012.

10 Michael Heatley, *Neil Young: In His Own Words* (London, 1997), p. 46.

11 Ibid.

12 McDonough, *Shakey*, p. 128. Some of Young's comments suggest that he
    might have written a version of 'Cortez the Killer' in school: ibid., p. 491.
    Had Young written the song after the publication of Hugh Thomas's history
    Conquest: Montezuma, Cortés, and the Fall of Old Mexico (New York, 1994)
    he might have nuanced his portrait of the Spaniard, focusing more on the
    mysterious disappearance of the women in his life.

13 Ulrich Adelt, '"Hard to Say the Meaning": Neil Young's Enigmatic Songs of
    the 1970s', *Journal of Popular Music Studies*, XVII/2 (2005), p. 168.

14 Rogan, *Neil Young: Zero to Sixty*, p. 370.

15 Adelt, '"Hard to Say the Meaning"', p. 170. The reading of Young as a
    character in the song is given credence by his reflection in the final verse of
    'Hitchhiker', written in the mid-1970s but not included on a studio album
    until 2010's *Le Noise*.

16 By llama this journey would take about a year. Llamas tend only to carry
    children; the weight of a full-grown man would be too heavy, especially for
    such an epic journey.

17 See Ludvig Hertzberg, ed., *Jim Jarmusch: Interviews* (Jackson, MS, 2001), pp. 156,
    172. See also Neil Young, *Special Deluxe: A Memoir of Life and Cars* (New York,
    2014), p. 295.

18 James Mazzeo's artwork is full of reprises of *Zuma*, see
    www.jamesmazzeoartworks.com.
19 Heatley, *Neil Young: In His Own Words*, p. 59.

6 SONIC JOURNEYS

1   Daniel Lanois, *Le Noise* interview out-take, September 2010 (available on
    YouTube at the time of writing).
2   Charles Saufley, 'The Man with the Midas Touch', *Premier Guitar* (21
    September 2010), www.premierguitar.com (accessed January 2015).
3   Jimmy McDonough, *Shakey: Neil Young's Biography* (New York, 2002), p. 75.
4   Jas Obrecht, 'Neil Young: In the Eye of the Hurricane', *Guitar Player* (March
    1992), p. 52. See also Larry Cragg, 'All the Young Tubes', *Guitar Player* (March
    1992), pp. 50–51; and McDonough, *Shakey*, pp. 7–8.
5   Obrecht, 'Neil Young: In the Eye of the Hurricane', p. 55.
6   Hank Harrison, *The Dead Book: A Social History of the Haight-Ashbury
    Experience* (San Francisco, CA, 1973), p. 42.
7   Ibid., p. 43.
8   Albin J. Zak III, 'Bob Dylan and Jimi Hendrix: Juxtaposition and
    Transformation "All Along the Watchtower"', *Journal of the American
    Musicological Society*, LVII/3 (Fall 2004), p. 600.
9   See Mark Rowland, 'Cruise Control: Neil Young's Lonesome Drive', *Musician*
    (June 1988), pp. 63–74. Young discussed his post-polio condition and the
    importance of physical training in his 1988 Vox Pop Raw & Uncooked
    interview.
10 Sheila Whiteley, 'Progressive Rock and Psychedelic Coding in the Work of
    Jimi Hendrix', *Popular Music*, IX/1 (January 1990), p. 46.
11 Ibid., p. 38.
12 Ibid., p. 57.
13 Ibid., p. 46; Richard Keena-Levin, 'Jimi Hendrix', *Popular Music*, X/1 (January
    1991), p. 90.
14 William Echard, *Neil Young and the Poetics of Energy* (Bloomington, IN, 2005), pp.
    155, 157. Young stresses that 'I don't think I have to break a guitar to get a violent
    sound out of it': Obrecht, 'Neil Young: In the Eye of the Hurricane', p. 48.
15 For Devo's philosophy see Jade Dellinger, *We Are Devo! Are We Not Men?*
    (San Francisco, CA, 2003).
16 For Young on Sonic Youth see David Fricke, 'New World Order', *Melody Maker*
    (30 November 1991), pp. 24–5.
17 Quoted in Steve Martin, 'The God Father of Grunge Rock', *Pulse!* (December

1991), available at www.hyperrust.org (accessed January 2015).

18 Quoted in David Fricke, 'New World Order', *Melody Maker* (30 November 1991), pp. 24–5. For this quotation and a perceptive analysis of *Arc* see Echard, *Neil Young and the Poetics of Energy*, pp. 100–107.

19 Martin, 'The God Father of Grunge Rock'. When Young was inducted into the Rock and Roll Hall of Fame in 1995 he thanked Cobain for helping him to renew his musical commitment. Interestingly, psychedelic rockers The Flaming Lips' performance of 'A Day in the Life' at the 2012 Bridge School Benefit concert was not as radical a reworking of The Beatles' song as Young's version on his 2009 European tour.

20 McDonough, *Shakey*, p. 650.

21 Steve Sutherland, 'Reflective Glory', NME (15 July 1995), reprinted in NME (19 July 2014), pp. 40–43. For another positive review of the collaboration see Christopher John Farley, 'Neil Young, Gifted and Back', *Time* (3 July 1995), p. 56.

22 Echard, *Neil Young and the Poetics of Energy*, p. 26.

23 Michael Heatley, *Neil Young: In His Own Words* (London, 1997), pp. 44, 45.

24 Ibid., p. 23.

25 For discussion of the Geffen label and *Trans* see Fred Goodman, *The Mansion on the Hill: Dylan, Young, Geffen, Springsteen, and the Head-on Collision of Rock and Commerce* (New York, 1997), pp. 356–8.

26 McDonough, *Shakey*, p. 553.

27 George McKay, *Shakin' All Over: Popular Music and Disability* (Ann Arbor, MI, 2013), p. 64.

28 Echard, *Neil Young and the Poetics of Energy*, p. 82.

29 Neil Young, *Waging Heavy Peace* (New York, 2012), p. 93.

30 Young quotation, 11 May 2011, www.ponoworldtimes.com (accessed December 2014).

31 For a sceptical attitude see Bob Lefsetz, 'Neil Young's Pono Music Service Relies on Outdated Model that Trades on Fame', *Variety* (2 May 2014), www.variety.com (accessed December 2014).

32 We see this nostalgia for an ideal lost sound in a reflective passage in Neil Young, *Special Deluxe: A Memoir of Life and Cars* (New York, 2014), pp. 126–7. For Jack White's comments see 'The Big Interview with Dan Rather', AXSTV, (broadcast 17 September 2014).

33 See Young's presentation of Pono at Dreamforce '14 (16 October 2014) and his conversation with Charlie Rose. The latter was broadcast on PBS on 30 October 2014.

CONCLUSION: HUMAN HIGHWAY

1 Dave Zimmer, *Crosby, Stills & Nash: The Biography* (Cambridge, MA, 2008), p. 180.
2 Graham Nash, *Wild Tales: A Rock and Roll Life* (New York, 2013), p. 209.
3 Ibid., p. 210.
4 Young was also sceptical about the size of the stadia: see Neil Young, *Special Deluxe: A Memoir of Life and Cars* (New York, 2014), pp. 193–4.
5 Zimmer, *Crosby, Stills & Nash*, p. 194. For Young's comments on the CSNY 1974 tour see Cameron Crowe, 'Neil Young: The Last American Hero', *Rolling Stone* (8 February 1979), in Rolling Stone, *Neil Young: The Rolling Stone Files*, introduction by Holly George-Warren (New York, 1994), p. 188.
6 The telegram was sent on or around 21 July 1976. See Johnny Rogan, *Neil Young: Zero to Sixty – A Critical Biography* (London, 2000), p. 404. Stills did not play well on the tour, but a 'raw throat' might have been the real reason that Young pulled out: see *Rolling Stone Files*, pp. 147–8.
7 For a discussion of *Living with War* in the context of other music criticizing the Bush administration see Dorian Lynskey, *33 Revolutions Per Minute: A History of Protest Songs* (London, 2010), pp. 667–80. Young spoke about the conception and writing process of *Living with War* in an interview with Charlie Rose, broadcast on PBS on 17 July 2008.
8 Young's radio interview with Howard Stern and his appearance on *The Colbert Report*, both on 14 October 2014.
9 *Late Night with Jimmy Fallon*, 29 November 2010; and *The Tonight Show*, 7 July 2014.
10 *The Tonight Show*, 4 February 2015. Young also performed 'Who's Gonna Stand Up?' on this show, backed by The Roots.

BIBLIOGRAPHY

NEIL YOUNG BOOKS

Bielen, Ken, *The Words and Music of Neil Young* (Westport, CT, 2008)

Boyd, Glenn, *Neil Young FAQ* (Milwaukee, WI, 2012)

Chong, Kevin, *Neil Young Nation: A Quest, An Obsession (and a True Story)* (Vancouver, 2005)

Clark, Tom, *Neil Young* (Toronto, 1971)

Downing, David, *A Dreamer of Pictures: Neil Young, The Man and His Music* (London, 1995)

Dufrechou, Carole, *Neil Young* (New York, 1978)

Durchholz, Daniel and Gary Graff, *Neil Young: Long May You Run – The Illustrated History* (Minneapolis, MN, 2010)

Dysart, Joshua, *Neil Young's Greendale* (New York, 2010)

Echard, William, *Neil Young and the Poetics of Energy* (Bloomington, IN, 2005)

Einarson, John, *Neil Young: Don't Be Denied – The Canadian Years* (Ketchum, IN, [1993] 2012)

Heatley, Michael, *Neil Young: His Life and Music* (London, [1994] 1999)

—, *Neil Young: In His Own Words* (London, 1997)

Jenkins, Alan, ed., *On a Journey through the Past* (Bridgend, 1994)

Long, Peter, *Ghosts on the Road: Neil Young in Concert, 1961–2006* (London, [1996] 2007)

McDonough, Jimmy, *Shakey: Neil Young's Biography* (New York, 2002)

Rogan, Johnny, *The Complete Guide to the Music of Neil Young*, ed. Chris Charlesworth (London, 1996)

—, *Neil Young: Zero to Sixty – A Critical Biography* (London, 2000)

Rolling Stone, *Neil Young: The Rolling Stone Files*, introduction by Holly George-Warren (New York, 1994)

Simmons, Sylvie, *Neil Young: Reflections in Broken Glass* (Edinburgh, 2003)

Williams, Paul, *Neil Young Love to Burn: 30 Years of Speaking Out* (London, 1997)

Williamson, Nigel, *Neil Young: Stories behind the Songs, 1966–1992* (London, 2010)

Wilson, Sharry, *Young Neil: The Sugar Mountain Years* (Toronto, 2014)

Young, Astrid, *Being Young: Scott, Neil and Me* (London, Ontario, [2007] 2009)

Young, Neil, *Waging Heavy Peace* (New York, 2012)

—, *Special Deluxe: A Memoir of Life and Cars* (New York, 2014)

Young, Scott, *Neil and Me* (Toronto, [1984] 2009)

OTHER BOOKS

Bidini, David, *Writing Gordon Lightfoot: The Man, the Music, and the World in 1972* (Toronto, 2011)

Bone, Martyn, *The Postsouthern Sense of Place in Contemporary Fiction* (Baton Rouge, LA, 2014)

Braunstein, Peter, and Michael William Doyle, eds, *Imagine Nation: The American Counterculture of the 1960s and '70s* (London, 2002)

Browne, David, *Fire and Rain: The Beatles, Simon & Garfunkel, James Taylor, CSNY and the Lost Story of 1970* (Cambridge, MA, 2011)

Collins, Maynard, *Lightfoot: If You Could Read His Mind* (Toronto, 1988)

Connell, John, and Chris Gibson, *Sound Tracks: Popular Music, Identity and Place* (London, 2002)

Crosby, David, *Long Time Gone: The Autobiography of David Crosby* (New York, 2008)

DeKay, William, *Down Home: A Journey into Rural Canada* (Toronto, 1997)

Dellinger, Jade, *We Are Devo!: Are We Not Men?* (San Francisco, CA, 2008)

Diamond, Beverley, and Robert Witmer, eds, *Canadian Music: Issues of Hegemony and Identity* (Toronto, 1994)

Doggett, Peter, *Are You Ready for the Country: Elvis, Dylan, Parsons and the Roots of Country Rock* (New York, 2000)

Einarson, John, *Shakin' All Over: The Winnipeg Sixties Rock Scene* (Winnipeg, 1987)

—, *Desperados: The Roots of Country Rock* (New York, 2001)

—, *Made in Manitoba: A Musical Legacy* (Winnipeg, 2005)

—, *Four Strong Winds: Ian and Sylvia* (Toronto, 2011)

—, and Richie Furay, *For What it's Worth: The Story of Buffalo Springfield* (Lanham, MD, 1997)

Fawcett, Anthony, and Charles White III, *California Rock California Sound* (London, 1978)

Fetherling, Douglas, *Some Day Soon: Essays on Canadian Songwriters* (Dallas, TX, 1991)

Gleason, Ralph J., *The Jefferson Airplane and the San Francisco Sound* (New York, 1969)

Goodman, Fred, *The Mansion on the Hill: Dylan, Young, Geffen, Springsteen, and the Head-on Collision of Rock and Commerce* (New York, 1997)

Greenfield, Robert, *The Last Sultan: The Life and Times of Ahmet Ertegun* (New York, 2011)

Guralnick, Peter, *Lost Highway: Journeys and Arrivals of American Music* (Boston, MA, 1979)

Harrison, Hank, *The Dead Book: A Social History of the Haight-Ashbury Experience* (San Francisco, CA, 1973)

Haslam, Gerald W., *Workin' Man Blues: Country Music in California* (Berkeley, CA, 1999)

Hegarty, Paul, and Martin Halliwell, *Beyond and Before: Progressive Rock since the 1960s* (New York, 2011)

Hemphill, Paul, *The Nashville Sound: Bright Lights and Country Music* (New York, 1970)

Henderson, Stuart, *Making the Scene: Yorkville and Hip Toronto in the 1960s* (Toronto, 2011)

Hertzberg, Ludvig, ed., *Jim Jarmusch: Interviews* (Jackson, MS, 2001)

Hoskyns, Barney, *Across the Great Divide: The Band and America* (London, 1993)

—, *Hotel California: Singer-songwriters and Cocaine Cowboys in the LA Canyons 1967–1976* (Hoboken, NJ, 2007)

Hurst, Jack, *Grand Ole Opry* (New York, 1975)

Jenkins, Philip, *Decade of Nightmares: The End of the Sixties and the Making of Eighties America* (Oxford, 2008)

Jennings, Nicholas, *Before the Gold Rush: Flashbacks to the Dawn of the Canadian Sound* (Toronto, 1997)

Kapsis, Robert E., *Jonathan Demme: Interviews* (Oxford, 2008)

Kemp, Mark, *Dixie Lullaby: A Story of Music, Race and New Beginnings in a New South* (Athens, GA, 2004)

Kostash, Myrna, *Long Way from Home: The Story of the Sixties Generation in Canada* (Toronto, 1980)

Kubernik, Harvey, *Canyon and Dreams: The Magic and the Music of Laurel Canyon* (New York, 2012)

Lynskey, Dorian, *33 Revolutions Per Minute: A History of Protest Songs* (London, 2010)

McKay, George, *Shakin' All Over: Popular Music and Disability* (Ann Arbor, MI, 2013)

McNult, Randy, *Guitar Towns: A Journey to the Crossroads of Rock 'n' Roll* (Bloomington, IN, 2002)

Malone, Bill C., and David Stricklin, *Southern Music/American Music* (Lexington, KY, [1979] 2003)

Marcus, Greil, *Like a Rolling Stone: Bob Dylan at the Crossroads* (London, 2006)

Melhuish, Martin, *Heart of Gold: Thirty Years of Canadian Pop Music* (Toronto, 1983)

Mitchell, Gillian, *The North American Folk Music Revival: Nation and Identity in the United States and Canada, 1945–1980* (Aldershot, 2007)

Monk, Katherine, *Joni: The Creative Odyssey of Joni Mitchell* (London, 2012)

Nash, Graham, *Wild Tales: A Rock and Roll Life* (New York, 2013)

Neal, Jocelyn R., *Country Music: A Cultural and Stylistic History* (New York, 2013)

Neely, Kim, *Five against One: The Pearl Jam Story* (London, 1998)

Odom, Gene, with Frank Dorman, *Lynyrd Skynyrd: Remembering the Free Birds of Southern Rock* (New York, 2002)

Orman, John, *The Politics of Rock Music* (Chicago, IL, 1984)

Palaeologu, M. Athena, ed., *The Sixties in Canada: A Turbulent and Creative Decade* (Montreal, 2009)

Palmer, Bryan D., *Canada's 1960s: The Ironies of Identity in a Rebellious Era* (Toronto, 2009)

Peterson, Richard A., *Creating Country Music: Fabricating Authenticity* (Chicago, IL, 1997)

Priore, Domenic, *Riot on Sunset Strip: Strip: Rock 'n' Roll's Last Stand in Hollywood* (London, 2007)

Ritter, Jonathan, and J. Martin Daughtry, eds, *Music in a Post-9/11 World* (London, 2007)

Rodnitzsky, Jerome L., *Minstrels of the Dawn: The Folk-Protest Singer as a Cultural Hero* (Chicago, IL, 1976)

Rogers, Jimmie N., *The Country Music Message: All about Lovin' and Livin'* (Englewood Cliffs, NJ, 1983)

Ronstadt, Linda, *Simple Dreams: A Musical Memoir* (New York, 2013)

Schneider, Jason, *Whispering Pines: The Northern Roots of American Music – From Hank Snow to The Band* (Toronto, 2009)

Selvin, Joel, *Monterey Pop: June 16–18, 1967* (San Francisco, CA, 1992)

Shaw, Arnold, *The Rock Revolution* (New York, 1971)

Starr, Kevin, *Coast of Dreams: California on the Edge, 1990–2003* (New York, 2004)

—, *Golden Dreams: California in an Age of Abundance, 1950–1963* (New York, 2011)

Streissguth, Michael, *Outlaw: Waylon, Willie, Kris, and the Renegades of Nashville* (New York, 2013)

Thompson, Dave, *Hearts of Darkness: James Taylor, Jackson Browne, Cat Stevens, and the Unlikely Rise of the Singer-Songwriter* (London, 2012)

Unterberger, Richie, *Turn! Turn! Turn! The '60s Folk-rock Revolution* (San Francisco, CA, 2002)

Walker, Michael, *Laurel Canyon: The Inside Story of Rock-and-roll's Legendary Neighborhood* (London, 2007)

Whiting, Cécile, *Pop LA: Art and the City in the 1960s* (Berkeley, CA, 2008)

Wilentz, Sean, *Bob Dylan in America* (London, 2010)

Willman, Chris, *Rednecks and Bluenecks: The Politics of Country Music* (New York, 2005)

Zimmer, Dave, *Four Way Street: The Crosby, Stills, Nash & Young Reader* (Cambridge, MA, 2004)

—, *Crosby, Stills & Nash: The Biography* (Cambridge, MA, 2008)

Zimmerman, Nadya, *Counterculture Kaleidoscope: Musical and Cultural Perspectives on Late Sixties San Francisco* (Ann Arbor, MI, 2008)

ARTICLES

Adelt, Ulrich, '"Hard to Say the Meaning": Neil Young's Enigmatic Songs of the 1970s', *Journal of Popular Music Studies*, XVII/2 (2005), pp. 162–74

Bienstock, Richard, 'Rider on the Storm', *Guitar World Acoustic* (December 2005), pp. 26–30

Bindas, Kenneth J. and Craig Houston, '"Takin' Care of Business": Rock Music, Vietnam and the Protest Myth', *The Historian*, LII/1 (November 1989), pp. 1–23

Bonner, Michael, 'A Fork in the Road', *Uncut*, 212 (January 2015), pp. 44–51

Cocks, Jay, 'Dylan and Young on the Road', *Time* (6 November 1978), p. 89

Echard, William, 'An Analysis of Neil Young's "Powderfinger" Based on Mark Johnson's Image Schemata', *Popular Music*, XVIII/1 (January 1999), pp. 133–44

Farley, Christopher John, 'Neil Young, Gifted and Back', *Time* (3 July 1995), p. 56

Flanagan, Bill, 'The Real Neil Young Stands Up', *Musician*, 85 (November 1985), p. 32

Fricke, David, 'New World Order', *Melody Maker* (30 November 1991), pp. 24–5

Graff, Gary, 'Neil Young', *Guitar World* (June 1993; reproduced in May 1995), pp. 96–7

Grant, Barry K., '"Across the Great Divide": Imitation and Inflection in Canadian Rock Music', *Journal of Canadian Studies*, 21 (Spring 1986), pp. 116–27

Keena-Levin, Richard, 'Jimi Hendrix', *Popular Music*, X/1 (January 1991), pp. 89–91

Kent, Nick, 'The Young Will Run and Run', *Vox* (November 1990), www.rocksbackpages.com

Lynskey, Dorian, 'Neil Young's Ohio – The Greatest Protest Record', *The Guardian* (6 May 2010)

McDonough, Jimmy, 'Fuckin' Up with Neil Young: Too Far Gone', *Village Voice Rock and Roll Quarterly* (Winter 1989), available at www.thrasherswheat.org, accessed May 2015

Obrecht, Jas, 'Neil Young: In the Eye of the Hurricane', *Guitar Player* (March 1992), pp. 47–56

Plasketes, George, 'Anthems, Antagonists, and Accents: The Beat and Off-Beat of the American South', *Studies in Popular Culture*, xix/2 (October 1996), pp. 197–215

Rodnitzky, Jerome L., 'The Decline of Contemporary Protest Music', *Popular Music and Society*, 1 (Fall 1971), pp. 44–50

Rowland, Mark, 'Cruise Control: Neil Young's Lonesome Drive', *Musician*, 116 (June 1988), pp. 63–74

Saufley, Charles, 'The Man with the Midas Touch', *Premier Guitar* (21 September 2010), www.premierguitar.com

Simpson, Dave, 'Raging in the Fee World: The Many Furies of Neil Young', *The Guardian* (23 June 2015)

Sorensen, Sue, 'David Byrne and Neil Young as Film Directors', *Studies in Popular Culture*, xxx/1 (Fall 2007), pp. 105–23

Stein, Isaac, 'Transformer Man: An Exploration of Disability in Neil Young's Life and Music', *Review of Disability Studies*, iv/2 (2008), www.rds.hawaii.edu

Sutherland, Steve, 'Reflective Glory', *New Musical Express* (15 July 1995); reprinted in *New Musical Express* (19 July 2014), pp. 40–43

'Tin Soldiers and Nixon Coming', *Rolling Stone*, 61 (25 June 1970), p. 9

Whiteley, Sheila, 'Progressive Rock and Psychedelic Coding in the Work of Jimi Hendrix', *Popular Music*, ix/1 (January 1990), pp. 37–60

Whitesell, Lloyd, 'Harmonic Palette in Early Joni Mitchell', *Popular Music*, xxi/2 (May 2002), pp. 173–93

Wright, Robert A., '"Dream, Comfort, Memory, Despair": Canadian Popular Musicians and the Dilemma of Nationalism, 1968–1972', *Journal of Canadian Studies*, xxii/4 (1987), pp. 27–43; reprinted in *Canadian Music: Issues of Hegemony and Identity*, ed. Beverley Diamond and Robert Witmer (Toronto, 1994), pp. 283–301.

Zak, Albin J. iii, 'Bob Dylan and Jimi Hendrix: Juxtaposition and Transformation "All along the Watchtower"', *Journal of the American Musicological Society*, lvii/3 (Fall 2004), pp. 599–644

DISCOGRAPHY

STUDIO AND LIVE ALBUMS AS A RECORDING ARTIST

Neil Young (Reprise, 1968)

Everybody Knows This Is Nowhere (with Crazy Horse, Reprise, 1969)

After the Gold Rush (Reprise, 1970)

Harvest (Reprise, 1972)

Time Fades Away (Reprise, 1973)

On the Beach (Reprise, 1974)

Tonight's the Night (Reprise, 1975)

Zuma (with Crazy Horse, Reprise, 1975)

American Stars 'n Bars (with Crazy Horse, Reprise, 1977)

Decade (Reprise, 1977)

Comes a Time (Reprise, 1978)

Rust Never Sleeps (with Crazy Horse, Reprise, 1979)

Live Rust (live) (with Crazy Horse, Reprise, 1979)

Hawks & Doves (Reprise, 1980)

Re-ac-tor (with Crazy Horse, Reprise, 1981)

Trans (Geffen, 1982)

Everybody's Rockin' (with The Shocking Pinks, Geffen, 1983)

Old Ways (Geffen, 1985)

Landing on Water (Geffen, 1986)

Life (with Crazy Horse, Geffen, 1987)

This Note's for You (with the Bluenotes, Reprise, 1988)

Eldorado (Reprise, 1989; only released in Japan and Australia)

Freedom (Reprise, 1989)

Ragged Glory (with Crazy Horse, Reprise, 1990)

Arc/Weld (live) (with Crazy Horse, Reprise, 1991)

Harvest Moon (Reprise, 1992)

Unplugged (live) (Reprise, 1993)

Sleeps with Angels (with Crazy Horse, Reprise, 1994)

Mirror Ball (with Pearl Jam, Reprise, 1995)

Broken Arrow (with Crazy Horse, Reprise, 1996)
Year of the Horse (live) (with Crazy Horse, Reprise, 1997)
Silver & Gold (Reprise, 2000)
Are You Passionate? (Reprise, 2002)
Greendale (with Crazy Horse, Warner, 2003)
Greatest Hits (Reprise, 2004)
Prairie Wind (Reprise, 2005)
Living with War (Reprise, 2006)
Chrome Dreams II (Reprise, 2007)
Fork in the Road (Reprise, 2009)
Le Noise (Reprise, 2010)
Americana (with Crazy Horse, Reprise, 2012)
Psychedelic Pill (with Crazy Horse, Reprise, 2012)
A Letter Home (Reprise, 2014; originally released on Third Man Records)
Storytone (Reprise, 2014)
The Monsanto Years (with Promise of the Real, Reprise, 2015)

SOUNDTRACK ALBUMS

Journey through the Past (Reprise, 1972)
Dead Man (Warner, 1992)

ARCHIVES AND PERFORMANCE SERIES

Neil Young Archives Vol. 1: 1963–1972 (Reprise, 2009)
> This first volume of the planned five-volume *Archives* project spans Young's early songs with The Squires to the year that Young recorded his fourth solo album *Harvest*. It also contains a live solo performance at the Riverboat, Toronto, from February 1969.

Neil Young Archives Vol. 2: 1972–1982 (Reprise, forthcoming)
> The second volume is thought to include the unreleased albums *Homegrown* (1975) and *Chrome Dreams* (1977), plus the more obscure *Oceanside–Countryside* and tracks from CSNY's unfinished *Human Highway* album, in addition to Neil Young and Crazy Horse concerts in London and Japan from March 1976.

Live at the Fillmore East (March 1970 concert; released 2006. Also included on *Neil Young Archives Vol. 1*)

Sugar Mountain – Live at Canterbury House, 1968 (9–10 November 1968 concert; released 2008. Also included as a bonus disc on the DVD version of *Neil Young Archives Vol. 1*)

Live at Massey Hall 1971 (January 1971 concert; released 2009. Also included on *Neil Young Archives Vol. 1*)

Dreamin' Man Live '92 (various 1992 U.S. concerts; released 2009)

A Treasure (1984–5 tour with the International Harvesters; released 2011. The deluxe version contains video performances from the tour)

Neil Young Official Release Series Discs 1–4 (Reprise, 2012)

Neil Young Official Release Series Discs 5–8 (Reprise, 2014)

ALBUMS WITH BUFFALO SPRINGFIELD

Buffalo Springfield (Atco, 1967)

Young wrote five tracks on the debut Buffalo Springfield album: 'Nowadays Clancy Can't Even Sing', 'Flying on the Ground is Wrong' and 'Do I Have to Come Right Out and Say It' were sung by Richie Furay; 'Burned' and 'Out of My Mind' by Young.

Buffalo Springfield Again (Atco/Atlantic, 1967)

Young wrote and sung on three tracks: 'Mr Soul', 'Expecting to Fly' and 'Broken Arrow'.

Last Time Around (Atco, 1968)

Richie Furay sung Young's track 'On the Way Home' and the co-written track 'It's So Hard to Wait', while Young contributed just one song as writer and singer, 'I Am a Child'.

Buffalo Springfield (box set) (Rhino, 2001)

This four-CD box set contains 30 versions of Young's songs, together with three co-written songs. These include alternate versions of album tracks and some previously unreleased recordings.

ALBUMS AS CROSBY, STILLS, NASH & YOUNG

Déjà Vu (Atlantic, 1970)

Young contributed two tracks, 'Helpless' and the 'Country Girl' medley, and he co-wrote 'Everybody I Love You' with Stephen Stills.

4 Way Street (Atlantic, 1971)

This four-disc album includes the following Young songs: 'On the Way Home', 'Cowgirl in the Sand', 'Don't Let it Bring You Down', 'Southern Man' and 'Ohio'. The 1992 CD rerelease also includes the medley 'The Loner' / 'Cinnamon Girl' / 'Down by the River'.

American Dream (Atlantic, 1988)

Young featured prominently on this CSNY album and he was the driving force behind it. He wrote four tracks by himself, 'American Dream', 'Name of Love', 'This Old House' and 'Feel Your Love', and co-wrote 'Got it Made', 'Drivin' Thunder' and 'Night Song' with Stills.

Looking Forward (Reprise, 1999)

This first CSNY album for Reprise contains four Young tracks: 'Looking Forward', 'Slowpoke', 'Out of Control' and 'Queen of them All'.

Crosby, Stills & Nash (box set) (Atlantic, 1991)

This 77-song box set contains just two of Young's songs, 'Helpless' (1969) and 'Ohio' (1970), and a live version of the co-written 'Got it Made' (1989), sung by Stills at a concert held on 18 November 1989 at the United Nations General Assembly, New York.

CSNY 1974 (box set) (2014)

This four-CD/DVD box set documents CSNY's summer 1974 tour, featuring a large repertoire by Young and including unreleased tracks from the abandoned CSNY *Human Highway* album. The three CDs are packaged with a DVD of eight songs filmed at Capital Center, Landover, Maryland and Wembley Stadium, London. The Wembley concert of 14 September 1974 includes the unreleased 'Pushed it over the End', which Crosby rates as the most powerful of all Young's performances.

In addition, Atlantic released the CSNY compilation *So Far* in August 1974 (including the single of 'Ohio' and cover art by Joni Mitchell). The soundtrack album to accompany MGM's 1970 student film *The Strawberry Statement* includes two tracks by Young, 'Down by the River' and 'The Loner', plus 'Helpless' performed by CSNY and 'Long Time Gone' by CSN.

STILLS/YOUNG BAND

Long May You Run (Reprise, 1976)

This album contains four tracks by Stephen Stills and five written and sung by Young: 'Long May You Run', 'Midnight on the Bay', 'Ocean Girl', 'Let it Shine' and 'Fontainebleau'.

SINGLES

For a discography of Young's singles, from The Squires' only recorded single 'The Sultan' / 'Aurora' (released in September 1963) and Buffalo Springfield's first double A-side 'Nowadays Clancy Can't Sing' / 'Go and Say Goodbye' (August 1966), through Young's first solo single 'The Loner' / 'Sugar Mountain' (December 1968), up to the release of *Silver & Gold* (April 2000), see Johnny

Rogan, *Neil Young: Zero to Sixty* (London, 2000), pp. 690–94 (Rogan also provides an extensive list of bootlegs.) The book included in *Neil Young Archives Vol. 1* has detailed information of song recordings from July 1963 to May 1972.

CONCERTS

Major tours and high-profile concerts are listed in the Chronology. See the Sugar Mountain website (www.sugarmtn.org) for a comprehensive list of concerts, beginning with a 23 October 1968 show at The Bitter End, Greenwich Village (where Young opened for Joni Mitchell), through his CSN and Crazy Horse collaborations to the present.

Much of the data is drawn from Pete Long, *Ghosts on the Road: Neil Young in Concert, 1961–2006* (London, [1996] 2007).

Additional information is available on the following three websites: Neil Young Times, at www.neilyoung.com/news; the Thrasher's Wheat fansite, www.thrasherswheat.org; and the Neil Young Appreciation Society, www.nyas.org.uk (133 issues of the fanzine *Broken Arrow* were published between 1981 and 2014).

FILMOGRAPHY

NEIL YOUNG FILMS

Journey through the Past, dir. Neil Young (1972; also included on the DVD version of *Neil Young Archives Vol. 1*)

Rust Never Sleeps, dir. Neil Young (1979) with Crazy Horse

Human Highway, dir. Neil Young and Dean Stockwell (1982)

Neil Young in Berlin, dir. Michael Lindsay-Hogg (1983)

Solo Trans, dir. Hal Ashby (1984)

Live in a Rusted Out Garage, Showtime PPV broadcast (21 November 1986)

Rock at the Beach – Live, dir. Neil Young (1990)

Unplugged, dir. Beth McCarthy-Miller (1993)

Complex Sessions, dir. Jonathan Demme (1994) with Crazy Horse

Year of the Horse, dir. Jim Jarmusch (1997) with Crazy Horse

Neil Young: Silver and Gold, dir. L. A. Johnson (1999)

Road Rock/Red Rocks Live, dir. L. A. Johnson (2000)

Greendale, dir. Neil Young (2004) with Crazy Horse

Neil Young: Heart of Gold, dir. Jonathan Demme (2006)

Neil Young: Under Review, 1966–1975 (2006)

Neil Young: Under Review, 1976–2006 (2007)

Neil Young: Hot Summer Nights in London (1971 and 1976 concerts; released 2008)

CSNY/Déjà Vu, dir. Neil Young (2008)

Don't Be Denied, BBC documentary (31 October 2008)

Neil Young Trunk Show, dir. Jonathan Demme (2009)

A Day in the Life, BBC broadcast from Glastonbury Festival (26 June 2009)

Neil Young Journeys, dir. Jonathan Demme (2011)

Le Noise, dir. Adam Vollick (2011)

Neil Young's Western Heroes, dir. Alex Westbrook (2011)

ADDITIONAL FILMS

Celebration at Big Sur, dir. Baird Bryant and Johanna Demetrakas (20th Century
Fox, 1971, 2011)

This open-air concert held at the Esalen Institute, Big Sur, California,
13–14 September 1969, includes Young playing 'Sea of Madness' and an
incomplete version of 'Down By the River' with Crosby, Stills & Nash.

Woodstock: The Director's Cut, dir. Michael Wadleigh (Warner, 1970, 1994)

Young famously did not appear in the film of the 15–18 August 1969
Woodstock concert at his request, despite playing acoustic and electric sets
with Crosby, Stills & Nash.

The Last Waltz, dir. Martin Scorsese (United Artists, 1978, 2002)

The film of The Band's farewell concert features a solo performance of
Young singing 'Helpless'. His cover of Ian & Sylvia's 'Four Strong Winds',
his collaboration on 'Acadian Driftwood' with The Band and Joni Mitchell,
and two closing ensemble jams are only available on the remastered 2002
audio album.

'68, dir. Steven Kovacs (New World Pictures, 1988)

Young plays the motorbike salesman Westy in this twenty-year retrospective
fiction film, focusing on a Hungarian immigrant family in San Francisco
during 1968.

Bob Dylan 30th Anniversary Concert Celebration (Sony, 1993)

Young performed two Bob Dylan songs with Booker T. & the MG's at this
celebratory concert held at Madison Square Gardens on 16 October 1992:
'Just like Tom Thumb's Blues' and a Jimi Hendrix-style version of 'All along
the Watchtower'.

Live Aid (Woodcharm / Warner, 1985, 2004)

The 2004 four-DVD box set documenting the Live Aid concert at Wembley
Stadium, London and John F. Kennedy Stadium, Philadelphia on 13 July 1985
includes two tracks played by Young and the International Harvesters ('The
Needle and the Damage Done' and 'God's Perfect Plan'), but omits three
further songs ('Sugar Mountain', 'Helpless' and 'Powderfinger') and two
performed by CSNY ('Only Love Can Break Your Heart' and 'Daylight Again'
/ 'Find the Cost of Freedom').

Farm Aid 2001: A Concert for America (Image Entertainment, 2002)

This concert was held in Noblesville, Indiana, on 29 September 2001 and
features 'Don't Cry No Tears' (from *Zuma*) and 'When I Hold You in My
Arms' (from *Are You Passionate?*).

Farm Aid: 20th Anniversary Concert (Sony, 2008)

Filmed at the Tweeter Center, Chicago on 18 September 2005, this concert includes two Young solo tracks from *Prairie Wind*: 'When God Made Me' and 'This Old Guitar'.

Bridge School Benefit: 25th Anniversary Edition (Reprise, 2011)

This retrospective DVD only features one of Young's songs, a 1989 version of 'Crime in the City', but Young also accompanies REM on 'Country Feedback' from the 1998 concert. The CD of the concert contains a 1990 acoustic version of 'Love and Only Love' with Crazy Horse. The *Bridge School Benefit* DVD also includes 'The Bridge School Story' documentary.

ACKNOWLEDGEMENTS

Just like Neil Young's journeys, this book has many beginnings. The first of these was my initial immersion in Young's music during my undergraduate years. I would like to thank Adam Siviter and Simon Atkinson for sharing their musical interests with me in Exeter, and a fellow student called Clive for his blistering performance of 'Rockin' in the Free World' after months of giving the impression of being comatose. I shared music with another good friend, Clive Rex, during this time, even if I didn't quite equal his passion for Moby Grape.

My interest in Young really developed during my Nottingham postgraduate years, for which I would like to thank Ben Andrews, Colin Harrison, Paul Hegarty and Michael Hoar. The four of us saw the Trent FM Arena concert in Nottingham in June 2009, the only time that Young has played in the East Midlands. I owe the greatest debt to Michael, for his perceptive insights into lyrics I had usually misheard, for sharing such good times (including a great 2001 Neil Young and Crazy Horse show in Birmingham) and for making me laugh. I also want to thank Laraine Porter, who was there for me through this time. I'm glad we had the chance to go to the launch of Graham Nash's *Wild Tales* at the Library of Congress during the early stages of writing this book.

The concept for *Neil Young: American Traveller* stemmed from a late-night discussion of 'Ohio' with Robert Jones II and Michelle Houston in an upstairs room in Manchester in April 2012. My colleagues George Lewis and Brian Ward were there around the edges of the conversation, probably mockingly, so I will mention them too.

The writing of this book in 2013–14 was a period of turbulence for me. The one person who helped to kick it into life and to keep it moving is Alexandra Zagaria. A devotee of *Rolling Stone* and The Rolling Stones, we have drifted through some great NY conversations, even if she has yet to read that copy of Scott Young's *Scrubs on Skates*. The best parts of this book are better because of Alex.

I am very grateful to Jim Brown and Jennifer Kirkwood of Kelvin High School, Winnipeg, for contacting former pupil Laura Clark, who created the fantastic painting of Neil Young in repose with the plains of Manitoba in the background – an image that is proudly on display on the school wall. Trips to Canada in 2013 and 2014 gave me the opportunity to conduct research at Winnipeg and Calgary public libraries and the University of Toronto, to complement my work in the Performing Arts Reading Room at the Library of Congress. In this respect, my gratitude goes to the University of Leicester for supporting my research and writing over the last fifteen years and the Institute of the Americas, University College London, where I was a visiting professor during the writing of this book.

My thanks are also due to the following colleagues and friends who sent me extremely helpful comments on the typescript: Martyn Bone, Paul Hegarty, Rob Jones ii, Andy Mousley, Phil Shaw, Deborah Toner, Greg Walker, Adam Woods and Alex Zagaria, as well as to the Reverb series editor, John Scanlan, and Michael Leaman at Reaktion for their advice and encouragement in bringing this book to fruition. Finally, I would like to thank the bclc Choir of Tangjungpura University, who welcomed me to West Kalimantan with a special version of 'Heart of Gold' on my first visit to Borneo.

I write this on 12 November 2014, Neil Young's 69th birthday. I think he sent me a gift today in the shape of Rush's Geddy Lee, with whom I rode an escalator in Heathrow Airport. Thanks Neil.

PHOTO ACKNOWLEDGEMENTS

The author and the publishers wish to express their thanks to the below sources of illustrative material and / or permission to reproduce it:

12-Gauge Productions / Pandora / Kobal, 1995: p. 125; photograph by the author: pp. 30 (2014), 52 (2015), 97 (2011); art design by Gary Burden: p. 64; © Laura Clark 2005, courtesy of Kelvin High School, Winnipeg: p. 28; Corbis: pp. 75, 120 (Henry Diltz), 127 (Caterine Milinaire / Sygma), 145 (© Thierry Orban / Sygma); courtesy of the artist (Jeremy Deller) and The Modern Institute, Glasgow: p. 13; Getty Images: p. 157 (Douglas Gorenstein / © 2015 NBCUniversal / Getty Images); © Janice Heo 2010: p. 24; The Kobal Collection: pp. 45 (Paramount Classics), 85 (Paramount Classics / The Kobal Collection / Bob Vergara, 2005); © Bob Masse, 2004: p. 155; album artwork by James Mazzeo: p. 111; album artwork based on an image by James Mazzeo, art direction and design of the cover by Gary Burden and Jenice Heo for R. Twerk & Co.: p. 103; Redferns: pp. 61 (GAB Archive, 1968), 79 (Ed Perlstein, 1975); Rex / Shutterstock: p. 47 (Paramount Classics); photograph by Alexandra Zagaria, 2015: p. 147.

INDEX